SAFELY THROUGH THE FIRE

*For Myra,
my a TRUE
my FRIEND ! ! !
Love is the Answer —*

*Nirmala
(Claire Anderson)
1/30/18*

SAFELY THROUGH THE FIRE

▼

A Story of Love, Loss, and Rebirth

Claire Anderson

Writers Club Press

San Jose New York Lincoln Shanghai

Safely Through the Fire
A Story of Love, Loss, and Rebirth

Writers Club Press
an imprint of iUniverse.com, Inc.

For information address:
iUniverse.com, Inc.
5220 S 16th, Ste. 200
Lincoln, NE 68512
www.iuniverse.com

ISBN: 0-595-19138-X

Printed in the United States of America

This book
is lovingly dedicated
to the memory
of
William Earl Anderson
whose death by AIDS
on
September 27, 1992
provided me
with the priceless opportunity
to grow
in
love, understanding,
and hope.
And
to
His Holiness
Sri Ganapathi Sachchidananda Swamiji
Loving and Silent Teacher

*   *   *

Jaya Guru Datta

"Do not be afraid…
When you pass through the waters,
I will be with you.
When you pass through the rivers,
they will not sweep over you.
When you walk through the fire,
you will not be burned…"
—*Isaiah 43*

ACKNOWLEDGMENTS

This has been a most difficult page for me to write because in singling out the supportive people in this endeavor, I am apt to forget some of you. So I shall begin with this general acknowledgment and perhaps this will be enough. I want to thank a loving Universal Energy and its spiritual emissaries for their undying support of this project. Without their blessing, direction, and loving assistance, this book would never be. And to all the proofreaders, critics, visionaries, and others who encouraged me along the way, please know that I am grateful.

For the physical production of this book I am grateful to the following angel-people: to Chuck Moses, for the author photo that appears on the back cover; to Jim Nazaruk for much appreciated technical assistance; to Art Lafferty for his editing services; to George Fennel for the computer and for related assistance (and then there's Clippet!!!); and to the good folks at Writers Club Press. Thank-you all for making this dream a reality.

If I would single out the ones to whom I owe the deepest debt, it would be the players themselves—the Michaels and Toms, the Annas and the Billy's of the world who have drawn us irresistibly into the Search for Life's

Meaning. Because of them we Look—and because we Look…we Find. They are the True Heroes of this project. They are the Inspiration. They are our Hope.

Claire Anderson
Spring 2001

CONTENTS

FOREWORD

Should this work endure into an age when understanding, acceptance, and compassion are the rule of the day, I want the reader to know that there was a time in the history of mankind when it was not so. Against the dark social backdrop of fear, superstition, and intolerance, some souls shown as brilliant stars, reminding us that there was indeed a better way. My brother was such a Star. Within these pages I have offered the reader an opportunity to gaze upon the night sky of the disease called AIDS and to discover that, contrary to popular opinion, it is ablaze with the welcoming light of love, peace, and hope.

Claire Anderson
Spring 2001

INTRODUCTION

The parade was over.

The crowd of Memorial Day celebrants slowly gathered around the podium for the annual Memorial Day speech and laying of the laurel for Springvale's fallen sons and daughters.

"Springvale is coming out of the Dark Ages," Billy noted to the sister who accompanied him on this trip down memory lane. Neither of them had witnessed the festivities of the day in years. But it was THEIR parade. First as Scouts and then as players in the local marching band, they had done the route. And many times…

And now he was making the observation. Change was coming to this small lakeside community. "They're finally letting a woman make the Memorial Day speech." That was a fact. And it was definitely a step forward.

Anna and her brother listened for a few moments and then allowed the lure of the cemetery beyond to call them. "Let's go for a walk."

Little puffs of dust rose from their feet as they walked the familiar road. They followed its course as it lazily wound its way through the 'at rest' citizens of their hometown. The shade was cool. Geraniums fairly glowed in the late May sunshine. Engraved stones, polished and glistening in the sunlight surrounded them.

They knew where they were going. Gram and Grampa were buried in that far corner. And just beyond them was the small patch of ground their parents had purchased over 20 years ago. No marker graced the family plot. No one had dared to fill even one of the eight empty gravesites. Not yet at least.

Anna picked a dandelion and blew the tiny seedlings into the spring-time air.

"Don't you wonder," she said absently, "don't you wonder who will be the first one buried in here?"

She was unaware of the silence emanating from her companion at that moment. Or of how tense he had become.

She rambled on. "I think I would want to be buried here even though I'm married and I don't live here anymore…"

Within minutes, Anna had wandered off to look up names of anyone she might remember from her eighteen years as a Springvale citizen. College had delivered her years ago, but one never truly leaves the town he was born into. It was part of her make up. The stars and all. The meridi-ans. It was her entry point.

She posed the question and let it go that day. She would one day recall the brief exchange as a terrible blunder.

For HE knew full well who would be the first. And he knew he would be breaking the hapless news to their parents within the next few hours. It would be the hardest thing he would ever have to do.

He COULD tell HER, too. He could tell her FIRST and draw to him-self at least one ally before the anticipated storm. It might help to do it that way.

He opened his mouth to confess what he knew. And then looking at her in all her innocence, abandoned the exchange. There was no need to disturb her world. Not yet. She was too carefree and happy. Something HE would never be again.

No. Just let it go. Let it stay this way for a while, he thought. It will all come crashing down on her soon enough…

PART ONE

━━━━━━━━━━━▼━━━━━━━━━━━

THE LAST YEAR

CHAPTER ONE

---▼---

"WE ALL FALL DOWN"

"He whom the gods love dies young."
Callimachus, 3rd Century

Life's most difficult lessons never seem to wait until you are ready for them. Anna thought that they did until one dreaded Labor Day, when the sky fell, the sun grew dark, and she embarked upon a journey from which she would emerge completely altered. That day her cousin pulled her away from a family gathering, took her for a long walk, and as gently as any bearer of sad tidings could, told her something she had hoped she would never have to hear—"your brother has AIDS."

Anna would never forget the day when she first let the reality of those four words sink leadenly into her innermost being. She would always wonder what life would be like if that Labor Day had passed like any other and her oldest brother Billy was still in New York City, publishing books and waking up happy and healthy each morning in his apartment on West 24th Street. But that is something she would never know.

Billy once said of his battle with AIDS, "I am living the biggest event of my life." Anna lived that event with him, finding herself a reluctant character in what was, in reality, a very familiar tale. For it was not just her story but it was the tale of mankind's ongoing struggle to make sense of life's seeming tragedies and to emerge relatively unscathed from life's dark hours.

For Anna, the challenge could easily have taken any number of preferred forms. Surely there might have been an easier way to experience life's most poignant, yet basic lessons. But no...Her abrupt initiation into the quest of mankind began with four words, spoken in sadness, spoken with love...

"...Your brother has AIDS."

In the theater of her mind, Anna would replay that pivotal walk many times after hearing those words. It was one of those warm autumn days that feels like mid-July. The leaves were barely threatening to change color and fall to the ground. She knew it was inevitable—winter would come. The green life of summer had been giving way to the cold sleep of winter for as long as she could remember. Such life-death cycles seemed well and good in their natural setting. But in that instant of realizing what was being said to her, Anna was suddenly caught in its relentless, indifferent current. The inevitability of death and loss set up camp before her and dared her to banish it. It was Anna's turn to face mortality...and she wanted nothing to do with it.

As she and her cousin Elizabeth talked, Anna's eyes were drawn to the sight of a neighbor who was cutting the grass in his pasture field. She marveled that people in the world could be engaged in such mundane activities, while her little world tumbled down around her.

There were only two things she wanted to know in that devastating moment. There were many things that she was told. "He has known for almost two years...told your parents a year ago...wanted to be here to tell you himself...is too sick right now...Pneumocystis Carinii Pneumonia...sternum is cracked from the coughing...medication is bringing his fever down...controlling the cough...asked me to tell you...needs your support now more than ever..."

With each pass of the neighbor's mower the information came. With each pass of the neighbor's mower the shock and the grief settled in. With each pass, her two questions formed. "How long does he have?" and "What happens now?"

It was suddenly obvious. Life never WAS predictable, but it did carry that appearance. One could say with relative confidence that next week he would do this or that, and next year she would go here or there. One could fairly easily imagine his days following each other in a systematic way. The illusion of predictability had been shattered for Anna in those moments. Time became a priceless commodity. She wanted desperately for someone to take the palm of her hand, fill it with the remaining days of her brother's life, and tell her to spend it well.

Anna also wanted someone to tell her exactly how she could expect this situation to progress...She wanted specifics: like the fact that PCP would dog him for a year; that he would almost die from a freak diabetic condition, but survive somehow; that he WOULDN'T have tuberculosis when they said he did. She wanted to KNOW that he would continuously suffer from some debilitating digestive condition that would waste his body to nothing. She wanted to KNOW that he would miraculously survive for months with no T-cells and amaze everyone by walking around the day before he died.

Anna wanted to KNOW that she would be there with him at the end; that he would look at HER to say his last word; that his spirit would comfort her in his physical absence; and that she would more than survive all of this. She wanted no surprises. An uncertain future was intolerable. Anna wanted something she could hold onto.

No one stepped forward in those moments to offer her any of this information. So she fell into a heap like the proverbial Humpty Dumpty, cracked in a zillion places, waiting futilely for all the king's horses and all the king's men to come to the rescue...

No one came.

Monday gave way to Tuesday. Anna spent that long awful day completely indulging herself in self-pity and grief. She HAD to do this. She tortured herself with memories. There were happy memories of Christmases, birthdays, summer vacations, the year the neighbor kids had all played "The Man from U.N.C.L.E." until they ran out of plots. She was amazed at how much and how clearly she could recall.

With a quick probe of her memory, she was throwing him a surprise 21st birthday party again. Well, it was almost a surprise. Anna had needed to consult him about the guest list. But he had feigned wonder and amazement, and a good time was had by all.

With a new awareness, Anna realized that her instincts had been correct the year before, when she received only a hug and not her usual good-bye kiss from him after a short visit. Why the change? Her heart had stopped for a moment, frozen with fear that there was more to this. The truth of his condition had almost revealed itself. But she had quickly brushed the thought aside. And like their favorite literary character, Scarlett O'Hara, Anna determined she would think of that another day.

Along with these memories, Anna began to draw a picture of the future with an empty place where Billy should be. She imagined family reunions without the Cousins' Club president, holiday gatherings without his humor and cherished compliments, a Christmas card list without his name on it. She thought about the books he would never write and the doctoral degree he would never earn. What would happen to the family archives without its dedicated family historian to keep it in order? And she wondered—would she still be able to say she had three brothers? Or would it be that she HAD three brothers and now there were only two? It was maddening to think about. She did not WANT to think about ANY of it.

It was a grueling day. Anna hit her grief from every conceivable angle and cried until she thought the tears would never come again. Big brothers aren't supposed to die.

Anna did not realize it at the time—pain does not readily notice such things—but the process she was undergoing that bleak Tuesday was one of those hidden gifts that the realization of mortality seems to bring. It was the sudden ability to see—to see clearly—the value and dearness of another soul. All of the negatives melt away. Any complaints or shortcomings were suddenly immaterial.

Anna thought it regrettable that it should take the threat of tragedy to shift her into this awareness. It was almost as if the most important function of Billy's illness and potential loss was to wake her up. It was as if they were beckoning her to see beyond the petty activities of her daily life, to look deeply into someone's soul, and to truly see the beauty that was there.

Anna discovered many wonders about her brother that day. She became more fully aware of how much he meant to her and how much she had followed in his steps as they were growing up together. She began to list their similarities and was amazed at how many interests they had shared—music, books, drama…Life's sudden upheaval had unearthed a treasure. Her eyes were now open and there was much to see. Adversity had begun to work its magic and Anna knew what she had to do.

*   *   *

When Wednesday morning dawned, Anna had a new resolve. There was a precious soul in New York City. At that moment, he was not sure if his family would be rejecting him or not—a tragic dilemma unique to the AIDS patient. Billy knew that the news had been delivered and he was waiting. Who can say what kind of demons he may have been wrestling with as Anna was encountering her own? It was time to send the monsters home.

According to the phone bill, at 1:04 P.M. on that warm September afternoon, a determined sister and her dying brother reconnected in the strangest, most precarious relationship she had ever known. Anna was amazed at their conversation. The laughter. Now, where did THAT come from? And yet it was there. Chuckles were scattered throughout the whole conversation. "I have a greater chance of dying in a taxi cab on the streets of New York City than I do of dying of AIDS," Billy jokingly said. "I take my life into my own hands every time I get into one of those things!" In such a case Anna assured him she would be sure to refer to him as an AIDS "survivor." The blessed balm of humor did its healing work between them. Another gift, she suspected—sweet tears to follow the bitter ones.

With great relief Anna welcomed Billy back. The knowledge of his condition, and his decision to keep it from his family for a while had left a puzzling wall between them. For months she had felt like she couldn't reach him. And she had missed him. Now that all made sense and the wall was no longer necessary.

They talked about rocking chairs, too. They should all be able to sit together at the old folks home some day, rocking and reminiscing about old times, Anna had said. It is the way it should be. Billy's response to the rocking chairs brought Anna face to face with a side of him that she would see repeatedly throughout the course of his illness. It was a response of hope. Not a desperate hope, but a quiet, knowing sort of hope. "We still may get to do that," he said. "They are working on a cure, and there are so many prolonging things they can do now."

Anna's brother was NOT dead. That was certain. He was very much alive. His very being seemed to snap her out of the deep pit she had been threatening to occupy permanently. In the presence of such life, death seemed far away. There were things he was still going to do, places he would yet go, people he would yet meet.

That day the telephone became a sacred object, transmitting life and hope to a grief-stricken sister. If he was going to continue living, then so would she. The measure of a life need not be made in length of days, but rather, in the depth of the present experience. The choice is there. Perceive it as a trap—something to be resisted—or see it as an occasion to fly and experience everything possible. Life is today. It belongs to us all equally.

Use it well. This is the message that the person Anna had naively intended to comfort imparted into her being that day. And there it would remain.

As Anna moved on from that conversation, she knew she was going to be OK. They all were. It would not always be easy, but it would not be impossible either. She had her brother to share this with. She had been pleasantly surprised by this realization. She didn't have to miss him yet. They could do this together. She would draw from his courage and offer comfort and support in return. Each of them would do what they had to do and they would get through this.

In the meantime, death would just have wait. They still had some living to do.

CHAPTER TWO

▼

BLESSED INTRUDER

"Religion has taken our spirituality away from us.
AIDS is giving it back to us again."
George Coleman

In the weeks that passed, Billy's condition began to stabilize and he made plans to come home to celebrate his 38th birthday. What would normally have been a nice occasion to relax and get away from the usual routine became a double dilemma for Anna. It was not all so simple as gathering at the family homestead, watching him open a few gifts, watching him blow out a few candles, slapping a back or two, and then going home. Everything was different now. Maybe it shouldn't be, but it was.

For Anna—for them all—there was the obvious difficulty of realizing that this was probably the last birthday she would celebrate with him. She was not really comfortable with the idea of "the last" anything, let alone birthday. As October 13th approached, she deliberately kept her mind off the implications. Anna remained in full retreat, deciding she would do nothing differently. She did not usually buy gifts for her brothers or sisters. She rarely sent cards. Occasionally, she made a phone call to wish the celebrant a happy day. Many times she would call several days late. It was Anna's way.

For what indeed became her brother's last birthday, Anna did the usual. She was there. She watched him open cards and gifts. She celebrated. But there was no card from Anna. Only the usual wish for happiness on his special day. Perhaps she was trying to convince herself that this was like any other birthday and that many more would follow.

Maybe she was afraid he would accuse her of giving up on him if she broke with her tradition. Most likely, it was just another symptom of the denial that had settled in upon her. Anna was not sure of any of these things. What she DID know was that it was a deliberate act and it felt right. Anna's gift to Billy was to be herself. She could do nothing more and nothing less.

As difficult as it was to handle this last birthday celebration, it was nearly impossible for Anna to deal with what she then believed to be the physical threat of the AIDS virus in his system. The deadly intruder had been there all along. For more than a decade, Billy surmised, the virus had been residing in his body, subtly wreaking havoc on his immune system. But Anna had been blissfully ignorant. Now that she knew of its presence, she was, quite frankly, afraid.

Anna was not immune to all of the mass hysteria and paranoia floating about regarding this disease. The sphere of influence from which she drew her information was decidedly religious in nature, with a moral ax to grind. Anna knew AIDS to be a highly infectious and incurable disease. She understood the virus to be present in all body fluids, including tears. But she had come into possession of some of the reactionary literature—"The Alarming Truth about AIDS and YOU!" Such information was designed to cast doubt on the Center for Disease Control's findings concerning the viability of HIV—the virus that causes AIDS—outside of the body and the way AIDS could be transmitted from one person to another.

Their subtle conclusion was that anybody could catch it from anybody—
so beware! It was enough to alarm anyone.

Anna's imagination had gone wild. She envisioned her children dying
one by one from the dreaded disease, while she and her husband, in an
ever-weakening condition, tried to help them. The disaster she foresaw
would be the result of touching Billy, or breathing the air after he
coughed, or eating the cake after he blew out the candles. It was embar-
rassing, yet she was out of control. What if the medical experts were all
lying, as the backlash so fiendishly implied. What if they were all infected
already. They had crossed paths with Billy many times in the years since he
had become infected. But for some reason, just knowing made Anna feel
vulnerable.

The virus seemed to take on a personality of its own—an obsessed personality. She feared it was now hell-bent on revenge for being disturbed in
its personal torment of her brother's life—as if it resented her support of
him. After all, AIDS had been elevated to the unenviable status of "curse."
AIDS was popularly seen as an expression of the wrath of God. If God was
actually punishing Billy for his sexual orientation, could He not also
decide to punish HER for loving him anyway? Was she guilty of some
horrible sin for supporting her brother? Was she supposed to turn her
back on him? Could this virus succeed in isolating him from his loved
ones in his greatest time of need?

The battle stormed within her for days. Anna was totally embarrassed
and disappointed with her reaction to the thought of confronting AIDS
face to face. But sheer will power alone could not set her fears to rest. As it
turned out, experience became her kind and gentle teacher. What all of
Anna's mental processes failed to do, time and life itself were eventually
able to accomplish.

With all of her concerns and apprehensions yapping at her heels, Anna
shakily grasped the hand of a greater Force that day and stepped ever so
cautiously back into her brother's life. "I am here because I love you, Billy.
I am scared to death, but I have decided that it is worth the risk to be here.

If God himself should strike me dead on the spot, I would still choose to be with you today. I would give up my health and my future to make sure you are not alone. You are worth it."

Anna did not actually say these things but the thoughts were with her throughout the whole day. They talked together. He coughed, and she breathed the air. He blew out the candles, and she ate the cake. She embraced him. She kissed his cheek. And in so doing, Anna took her first tiny steps toward coming to terms with this disease. With great timidity she defied the forces that threatened to victimize her along with her brother. She shook a hesitant fist in the face of the condemning monster and emerged the victor. And she sensed with all of her heart that God smiled.

That day marked the beginning of a gradual yet definite transformation in Anna's thinking. Each time she subsequently faced and defied her fear of AIDS, she received new strength. AIDS lost its monster quality and she felt she began to understand it and its purpose here. AIDS was not a curse or something to be dreaded. AIDS was a messenger. AIDS was here to teach something important, if people would only listen. Anna listened. And she learned.

One test of Anna's learning came on a hot summer afternoon almost a year after Billy's death, when some old friends of her family stopped by for a casual visit. She knew the gentleman to be a bit hard-nosed, and brittlely moral and upright. He had been a fellow parishioner in a church they once belonged to. Though they had been out of touch with each other for years, he knew that Anna had lost a brother to AIDS the previous fall. She assumed he realized that she had experienced a great deal of pain in recovering from that loss; but then again, he had no way of knowing WHAT she had gone through or how it had affected her.

His curiosity finally got the best of him and he sincerely, though a bit insensitively asked, "Do you think AIDS is a curse?"

Anna knew from experience, that he was not referring to the so-called "innocent" victims of the disease, but to the plight of the homosexual community. The question presupposed God's wrath and willingness to inflict pain on his "erring" creatures. It was all too painfully familiar.

Anna doubted that he saw the look of determination that crossed her face at the prospect of challenging this common misconception about the disease—AND about GOD for that matter. She strongly suspected that if he had realized what he was opening himself up to, he might never have asked the question in the first place. She mustered her courage and gave him a reply he was not expecting. "Well, actually, I believe AIDS is a gift. The people I know who are dealing with AIDS are some of the most loving and spiritually aware people I have ever met..." Here the conversation suddenly, yet understandably veered away from the subject at hand, though there was so much more Anna could have said.

She was not sure which aspect of her statement had shut him down the quickest. Whether it was the idea of gay men with AIDS being spiritual loving people, or the implication she made that God bestowed a blessing when a curse was in order. Either idea could have been offensive to him. Or maybe, it was the realization that she had abandoned the standards that 'folks like us' were supposed to uphold that bothered him so. It didn't matter. Anna knew what she knew.

She and Billy had talked briefly at one time about this concept. His idea was simple and Anna wished many times that he would have said more. He said that AIDS was not a curse. "It is a wage." Her first thought upon hearing these words was that he was simply referring to the law of consequence—i.e., if a person steps off a cliff, he falls to his own harm. But he answered her question with an aura of dignity and self-respect that often led her to wonder if he had meant this in a broader sense.

She KNEW her brother accepted his own responsibility in contracting this disease. But wasn't there also a sense in which the disease he bore in his body was a wage society had helped him earn?...as well as earned for itself? Perhaps he HAD walked intentionally off of a perilous "cliff"; but there was also an undeniable sense in which he had been pushed. After all, he was not born hating himself—people taught him that. He had not come into this life fraught with intense feelings of guilt. Those were gifts from the religion they had grown up in. He was not born a tormented soul. Rather, throughout his days there had been no shortage of cultural 'claw' and 'fang' willing to tear him down, based on a single aspect of his entire being. Against impossible odds Anna's brother had lived as long and as well as he could. The breaking down of his immune system was but a natural consequence of believing the consuming voices that said he was "less"—less human, less spiritual, less loved.

Anna could say it. AIDS was not a curse—unless that is to say it was a curse that fear and disdain had placed upon minority segments of society. But it didn't have to be that way. Society WAS its 'brother's keeper'. It HAD to be. And AIDS was merely an insistent reminder of that fact. It called loudly from every sickbed, imploring the world To Love.

Anna's righteous friend did not hear any of those things that August afternoon. Sadly, he would probably live out his days smugly assuming that God had finally found a way to deal with the "gay problem" once and for all. That's the way some would see it. But for others, this microscopic organism had been able to accomplish the monumental task of melting hearts of stone and awakening within them the refreshing healing love the world so desperately needed. They knew…

…The "curse" was a "blessing"—in disguise.

Anna was completely oblivious to this when she faced AIDS for the first time at that final birthday celebration. But that was when the process began for her, and she would continue to reap the eternal benefits of AIDS' hidden gifts..

CHAPTER THREE

▼

RIDING THE ROLLER COASTER

"I see within the dark heart of this disease called AIDS,
a light of great brilliance, shining…shining…"
—from a letter written by Mark Hamilton

It seemed a silly thing to recall. But once, when Anna and her brother were very young, they rode the roller coaster at a nearby summer amusement park. Though they tried, they could not make the seat belt work, nor could they catch the attendant's eye to get his assistance. As the small train of cars left the station, they suspected they were about to experience something in a way few people ever had.

Their suspicions were realized as they flew down the first eternal hill and were then thrown into the bottom of the car. They tried at various points along the way to get back into their seats, failing each time. They finally gave up and finished the ride, knowing it was all happening out there somewhere, but too preoccupied with survival to ever really enjoy it. As Anna was soon to find out, this was what living with a brother who was living with AIDS was like. There were ups and downs; attempts to get one's bearings followed by sudden drops and turns; and finally, a resignation to hold onto one other and wait for the end.

As they moved into the winter months, Anna's life became an ongoing struggle to cope with the emotional upheaval that accompanied the varied reports of change in her brother's physical condition. She didn't know what she had expected. Billy had long since moved into the symptomatic stages of the disease's progression, but nothing had prepared her for the emotional wear and the mental uncertainty that went along with terminal illness. Anna was not directly responsible for her brother's physical care since he lived over 300 miles away, but she was still intimately tied to him and his sufferings.

There were easy days when she would actually begin to feel "normal," as if it were all a dream and life had never gone off track. His condition would become stable and in some areas he would even improve. AIDS was giving them a blessed reprieve. On those days, Anna could almost convince herself that she was doing pretty well, and that she could handle all of this with ease. "This isn't so bad," she would naively think.

These were the times it became easiest to toy with the thought that Billy might be able to hold his own indefinitely. And then the phone would ring—AIDS had lost its patience and slammed into their lives again. So what was a person supposed to do when the painful reality of impending doom settled in and she found to her dismay that she was dropping things or sweeping the same floor over and over again. What could she do when she found herself pacing frantically and then sitting in stony silence with her mind screaming, "This is it. He's not going to make it through this time…"

Anna found to her eternal amazement that her best hope of comfort lay in climbing out of the dust she had just been knocked into and easing her way back into the presence of the one who embodied this suffering. She called him. She called him again and again and again and again during those difficult days.

"So...how are you REALLY?" Anna would ask. And if he was able to talk, Billy would tell her all about it. And then they would chat about the doctors and the mean nurse that should be fired immediately and the cockroach on the wall and how he knew why there were bars on the windows in this hospital—the idea of jumping was far too tempting.

It wasn't always pleasant news, but it was never as bad to hear it from HIM as it was to get the word second-hand. Hearing his voice and letting him explain to her what his life was like during the low spots, reassured Anna that he was hanging in there and that he was by no means ready to give it all up.

In fact, it was during those times of direct verbal contact with him that Anna became acutely aware of a dimension of life she had barely paid attention to before. Somehow, Billy always ended up talking about his body as if it were an old Ford giving him some trouble. He would spell out his plans to take it in to the mechanics. He counted on them to diagnose the immediate problem and have him back on the road again before too long.

It was perfectly obvious though that HE was not the old Ford. He just used it to get around. This comforted her. Somehow, Anna kept getting the feeling that there was nothing really wrong with Billy. It was true that his body was caving in around him, but what she was seeing was something deeper—something totally separate from IV's, medication, and disease. What she kept seeing was Life in its purest form—complete, unchanging, and eternal.

The strength of that Life within him often led her to experience confusion whenever people asked her how Billy was doing. Anna assumed they were interested to hear of his physical progress or perhaps how he was taking it all. But SHE wanted to tell people that he was fine. She wanted them to realize that HE was completely whole, vibrant, and healthy. For HE was.

The destructive force of HIV in Billy's physical body was pathetically powerless in its attempt to seize the real HIM. In fact, the sufferings served rather to fuel the fires of Life within him. Anna tried at one point to convey this insight by writing a Scripture in a card she sent him. It said that though outwardly we might be wasting away, yet inwardly we were being renewed every day, and that these temporary troubles were achieving a great 'glory' for us, that would far outweigh any of our sufferings. Months later, as she heard those words being read at his funeral—words he himself had carefully selected—she knew he had understood.

Unfortunately, Anna still had to deal with the physical realities of her brother's disease. She was given an unexpected opportunity to face those frightening realities one week in early February. It was the time she came closest to experiencing the role of "AIDS caretaker." And it was the time she had to humbly admit her total dependence on others to meet Billy's physical needs.

That week, family obligations and her own short illness forced Anna's mother to reluctantly leave her post at her brother's side for a few days. With Billy alone in his apartment for the first time since an extended hospital stay in January, and being aware of his impossibly low T-cell count of 4, Anna felt a great deal of pressure to keep track of him. The first calls she made to him that week revealed he had developed a condition that was making it difficult for him to keep food down. They were attempting to locate a bed for him in the hospital, but to no avail. He seemed relatively calm about it. Once when she phoned him, he was on his hands and knees scrubbing the closet floor. Another time, he was assembling a bookcase he had recently acquired. Anna marveled that he could remain focused on such things.

SHE, on the other hand, was experiencing a great deal of anxiety and frustration at the situation. The man needed help. He needed tests and treatment. He needed someone to get him where he needed to go. Anna strained at the chains of the limitations that kept her from flying off to the city to take care of him herself. Responsibilities at home made it virtually impossible for her to go to him, but she had to admit that she did not WANT this job either. She did not want to feel this deep responsibility for his daily care. She looked all over inside herself and came up with zero. The amount of disquiet she experienced in those few days forced Anna to realize what she could NOT do for this person, though she loved him dearly. It was not easy to admit.

Over time, Anna became more gracious with herself. She was able to accept the fact that not being able to help him with his physical needs did not mean that she loved him any less. She made peace with the special role she did play in his life. She was there for him in her own unique way. There were certain thoughts and feelings he could best express to her. Secure bonds forged in childhood made this possible. Anna could freely offer him an open ear, understanding, and unconditional support. She played her role well, as did the others in his life who cared for him.

It seemed there was yet another invaluable lesson tied up in Anna's frustrations during those cold February days. Amidst all of the ranting and ravings about her own feelings of helplessness, Anna had failed to take into account the possibility that there might be someone in all of New York City who would actually care for her brother as much as SHE did.

For reasons known most fully to him, Billy had decided long before this, to keep his friends and his family separate. Though Anna had long been aware of his adopted lifestyle, she had very little specific knowledge of it, nor of the significant people in his life. BUT…this was all about to change.

It happened with few words. It happened as Billy nonchalantly informed her on a Tuesday afternoon that "my friend Mitch"—as he put it—had taken the morning off from work to take him to the hospital for tests; and that on Thursday, Glen was coming over to do his laundry. Though Anna had met Glen when she visited with Billy during a two-hour layover at the airport in July, she did not know him very well. She did not know who "my friend Mitch" was at all. She did not know in what capacity her brother knew either of them. All she knew was that they cared. Mitch had heard of her brother's need and had given up his morning to help meet that need. Glen was planning to undertake the humbling task of washing another person's clothes. And with those two small gestures of kindness they single-handedly chiseled a significant crack in the wall Anna's brother had built between his two worlds.

A brilliant light streamed through the gap that day—a strangely familiar light. Anna recognized it to be the very same light she carried within her. It radiated care and concern for a fellow human being. It originated in a common love for a common soul.

Anna didn't know if Mitch or Glen ever realized how their loving deeds sustained and supported her in HER hour of need. She didn't know if they realized how comforting it was for her to know that her brother was experiencing their loving support. Could they possibly know the calm that settled over her weary soul as they unwittingly took her place and finished the work she was unable to do?

Anna decided that day that if life was ever kind enough to bring her face to face with "my friend Mitch", she would tell him. She would let him know what it meant to her for him to wait endlessly in a crowded waiting room, reading month old magazines while his friend endured the discomfort and humiliation of those medical tests. If it were ever possible Anna would thank Glen someday for hanging around a stuffy laundry room, sorting and folding someone else's clothes. She would thank them both for loving him.

CHAPTER FOUR

▼

OF PHOTOGRAPHS AND VEILS

"Let me take a picture of you,
A memory for my hand;
Then I will see you again someday,
And I will smile"

Tucked away in the far corner of a dusty closet of the restored farmhouse where she lived, Anna kept a random collection of photo albums. There, neatly arranged, was the pictorial record of her personal journey through life. Scattered among the pages was an occasional snapshot that captured her brother with friends or family, sharing the moment with her—or a memory. No matter the pose, he was always her Billy.

At times the camera had been handed over to an innocent bystander who was obliged to snap a picture of the two of them together. Some of these were casual shots. Some were posed. Each one provided a slice of two lives that ran parallel, then separated for awhile, but found ways to cross again and again over the years. Anna loved these pictures and she found herself looking at them more often than she used to, and seeing more in them when she did.

The most meaningful of these photographs of the two of them was taken on a balmy Sunday afternoon in March. It was also the last photograph that was ever taken of Anna and her brother together. The occasion was their grandmother's 88th birthday. Billy had recovered sufficiently from his February troubles to make the trip back to Springvale to spend a few days with family. It was a cold but clear Sunday afternoon when the family gathered around its matriarch and wished her the best.

At one point in the din of the celebration, and midst the laughter, the singing, and the merry-making, Anna became painfully aware of her brother's silent form seated on the stairway overlooking the festivities. He was there, and yet he was miles away. He was in a personal battle with nameless ghosts that were trying to take him away from the life and the family he loved. His relaxed form could not hide the results of the ongoing battle raging within him—results that showed in his thin frame and tired face. He had been through so much. There was such a long way for him to go. But Anna was not really a part of any of it.

For all of her concern and care for his well-being, the silent glances she cast in his direction only reinforced the sense of distance she felt from him. She was an outsider—a mere observer of another's arduous journey. His sufferings were his. He was alone in his efforts. But it is not the way she wanted it to be. Anna wanted to be a part of it. Not that she felt she could be of any great help to HIM; but rather, she believed there was something hidden deep within his situation that could be of great benefit to HER. Anna needed something that he was experiencing. She did not know exactly what it was, but she did not want to be left out.

In a moment that encompassed a thousand thoughts, Anna found herself moving toward her brother. In slow motion she shoved her camera in the direction of her sister Karen and told her she wanted her to take a picture of them. Then she turned and seated herself two steps below her brother and began to smile. He turned his face to the waiting photographer and smiled, too. A bright flash from the camera in Karen's hands sealed that moment into form forever.

It was just a picture—a routine snap of the shutter. A candid shot taken of two party guests sharing a genial moment together. These things happened all the time, but something about this was very different.

Looking back, Anna wondered if the flash of the camera in this particular instance was some sort of pre-arranged signal that she and Billy had agreed upon at a time long ago and a place far away. For as the spots before her eyes cleared, a new awareness came over her. She was indeed a part of all of this. She was a part of HIM. Anna would later say it was at this moment that she entered spiritually into her brother's sufferings, and in so doing, gained access to the invaluable path of learning that lay hidden deep within them. Her journey would be her own, and she would find her own way, but her path became inseparably entwined with his, and the crisscrossing of their lives and experiences would continue long after his death.

It was not so readily obvious that Sunday afternoon, that things of such great significance were occurring. The most immediate reaction this innocent picture-taking brought about was tears. Anna had not seen or heard of her brother shedding any tears in regard to his situation. She was sure there were many, but he kept them neatly tucked away whenever she was around. That afternoon, however, he opened the inner doors and blessed Anna with the presence of the only tears she would see him shed throughout his whole ordeal.

"It's hard sometimes," he said through tear-filled eyes.

Anna's own tears soon followed. She searched for the right words, yet could only absently say, "I know what you mean." Realizing her mistake, she quickly rescinded the remark, and admitted she had no idea what he was going through.

Anna moved up a step closer to him. She hung her elbow over his right knee, and they sat there. They shared a sacred moment. They sealed a silent vow. And for a few precious moments, their spirits were one.

Billy finally broke the silence with some small talk. Anna asked him how much time he thought he had left. Billy surmised that some infection would finally conquer him during the coming winter. He was going to stay in New York for the time being. He humorously, yet emphatically restated his desire to be what he called 'morphined out of his mind' when he finally became terminal, and he summed up how they both felt when he concluded with a sigh and a wistful "I don't know."

The future seemed so desolate, so unpredictable. No one knew what it held for any of them. Anna was as unsuspecting as the rest to what was coming.

The mystery of what was happening on the stairs that day brought significant and immediate internal changes to Anna. She knew important things were transpiring deep within her when she was suddenly plagued with an impulsive and somewhat irrational urge to let her hair grow long. Where had this desire come from? And why? It had nothing to do with fashion. Anna had been happy with a short style for many years. This sudden need to be covered had come on as suddenly as Billy's tears. It made no sense to her at the time. All she knew was that she had to do it. Over the coming months Anna sought to understand the meaning behind the persistent urge. And she dutifully followed through on the impulse, plagued with impatience many times at how slow and drawn out the process was.

Drawing on the limited spiritual frame of reference she had worked with up to that point, Anna at first attributed this 'longing to be veiled,' as she came to see it, with the idea of blind submission. Anna assumed she might be being prompted to close her eyes to what was happening, to give up any notions she might have of understanding these events, and to blindly accept someone else's patent explanation for her brother's fate. "It doesn't have to make sense." She had heard this on more than one occasion.

She had also read from her Bible that a woman's hair was considered to be her "glory," and Anna toyed momentarily with the thought that she was finally stooping to the level of bribing God. Perhaps, if she grew her hair long enough, she might be helped over the difficult issues that surrounded her brother's circumstances, or maybe—if she were lucky—it would all just go away. Although Anna thought along these lines in an effort to explain the sudden changes she was experiencing, none of it rang true.

Like many of her convictions about truth and life, these ideas were beginning to fade away. For what Anna had not yet realized that day, was that the tenets of her personal faith, boxed so neatly in their appropriate places had just been yanked from their respective shelves and dumped on to the floor like so many jigsaw puzzles. The resulting confused mass of jumbled ideas was going to require all of her attention. It is no wonder she wanted to pull the shades of obscurity down around her and shield herself from everything but the task at hand. Anna was a butterfly in the making, willing the tresses down around her like a protective chrysalis. The old was passing away. The new was inescapably on its way.

The truth of the matter was that the faith system Anna had held so tightly onto since childhood could not satisfactorily accommodate her brother's situation, nor could it sustain her any longer through this ordeal. It offered her little more than comfortless platitudes and offered only conditional hope for Billy.

According to that system of thought, the most acceptable scenario for a gay man with AIDS was for him to repent, to publicly repudiate the gay lifestyle, and then to give the remaining days of his life to serving the church in some AIDS-related capacity, hopefully encouraging other lost and dying souls to mend their ways. For him to NOT follow this course was to open himself up to suspicion, judgment, or total rejection.

But things were not so cut and dried with Billy. He had not openly done any of these things, though Anna had quietly anticipated a time when he would. There were no tears of remorse, no self-flagellation. Nor was there anger or defiance propelling him into this 'refusal.' He simply WAS who he WAS, and no neat well-defined category could hold him. So here he was, single-handedly crushing Anna's expectations and luring her into uncharted territory where she would have to make her own way and find her own answers. She should have been angry, but she wasn't. Instead Anna loved him all the more.

In fact, over the course of time, it eventually dawned on her that in all of her fervor to place Billy in some suitable religious framework, she had failed to notice how effortlessly he fit into her own life already. She loved him. Plain and simple.

Anna had no great driving need to see him change. She had not set up any requirements he had to meet before she could love him. She liked him just fine—just the way he was. He was brilliant, and caring, and funny! and a true friend. Why should he be held to anyone else's expectations? Was it possible that Anna's frail human capacity to love far exceeded the compassionate heart of God? What kind of God was this, that he could cross his arms and turn his back on one of his beautiful creations, while this loving sister with her human limitations, could embrace him—all of him with all of his so-called 'short-comings'—in her hopelessly flawed arms?

People. It was people alone who could not accept him, she thought. And to back their prejudice, they had shamelessly put their words into the mouth of God and ruthlessly encouraged everyone to throw stones.

Anna could not do it anymore. She could not judge him. Nor could she join any longer in the deep concern that Billy might die before he got his life "straightened out." The Light within him was too bright. His very being exuded the most intense 'Stillness' Anna had ever witnessed. Billy had obviously come to terms with himself and made peace within his soul.

Anna did not see him writhing in guilt or begging a merciless God to change his situation. She had not heard him complaining though many would say he had ample reason. Maybe he HAD done these things at times. After all, they had both sprung from the same depleted spiritual soil. But somehow, in the course of his sufferings, Billy had found the dignity and self-acceptance—the peace and the self-respect—the 'God' Anna longed for. Somehow, in the most unlikely of all circumstances, Anna's brother had found a meaningful faith that worked. And now—because of him—so would she.

Could it all be so simple, she wondered. Could it be that her brother's purpose in these last months of his life was to bring enlightening shades of gray into Anna's black and white world—to show her the simple truth that love LOVES, and that acceptance ACCEPTS without condition, without judgment, and without needing its object to conform to inflexible standards.

"Come. I will show you a better way," Billy's life whispered that day on the stairs. Maybe no one else heard it. Maybe she was the only one who would receive the precious gift he would be giving in leaving his earthly life in this manner. It didn't really matter. Anna made her choice. She followed her heart. And finally—at last—she was on her way Home!

CHAPTER FIVE

▼

WHEN DREAMS ARE GONE

*"As i lay here wondering what to do with this short
occurrence called life, such as a musician who has played the
songs and no longer knows what to do with his instrument, i
realize that time is the only factor against me."*
—*bob goehring*

Billy was finally forced to leave his beloved New York City in July. He had
stayed as long as he could. Of course, he had access to the most advanced
medical treatments and procedures as long as he stayed. But the time had
now come when the doctors could offer him no more help than he was
already receiving. The life Billy had made for himself in the heart of the
Big Apple had come to an end.

Anna could not begin to imagine what this was like for him. Billy had
always loved the city and it was no surprise to her when he chose to make
it his home. He had stopped at the college to see her on his way through
to his new life in Manhattan early in the fall of her sophomore year. Anna

was practicing with the college choir for an upcoming Christmas concert, when he poked his head through the door and motioned for her to come to him.

He was young, enthusiastic, and so hopeful for the future. Anna was happy for him, yet she knew they would never have such free and easy access to each other ever again. It was sad and happy all mixed together as they said their good-byes with the strains of German Christmas carols floating into the hallway from the singers beyond the door. He walked away, stopping once to look back with a wave and a thoughtful smile. And then he was gone.

Now he was coming full circle, leaving the city behind and returning to the place where his life had begun. It was a much smaller circle than any had anticipated, and it was not easy for anyone.

"In July he refused to say 'good-bye' to us," Glen later wrote, filling in the gaps of Billy's story for her. "He said he'd be back in New York to pick some things up in August. Without saying anything, we all knew this wasn't going to happen. At the time, however, I don't think your brother had accepted his destiny."

Anna could not blame Billy for resisting his fate. Dreams die hard. But he finally did set his thoughts toward going home, and spending his last days with the ones who had launched him into life. Anna could tell that he needed to do it that way for his own sake; but something about him convinced her that he knew THEY needed HIM, also.

The boxes were packed up along with the dreams and the plans that could not be realized. The trip was made. The settling in was completed as well as could be under the circumstances. And it was there in the small Pennsylvania town where they played make-believe so many years earlier, that they would meet and laugh and remember, and soon say their final good-byes.

Good-bye. People say it so often, so easily. It means "so long," "see ya later," "we'll meet for coffee tomorrow morning." They say it lovingly, tenderly, and sometimes angrily. But no one ever wanted to say it FINALLY.

That final good-bye waited silently behind her left shoulder where she could not see it. She knew it was there. She knew she would have to deal with it sometime. But Anna left it sitting silently in the shadows, dusty and unattended for as long as possible. Never mind that the day was rapidly approaching when the neglected moment would insist on being recognized—when it would clamor into the foreground, stand before her and say, "Now is the time."

For she was now entangled in a new dilemma. In all of the time Anna was able to visit Billy after he moved home, she found she could never quite find a way to bring up the things she wanted to say to him before he died. So many final things to talk about, but how to start? She needn't have worried. As it turned out, it was Billy himself who called for her. He was the one to initiate the conversation she had only fumbled at.

Her opportunity came on a quiet Sunday afternoon in early September during a visit with him and the family. It was a pleasant day. Gathered around the kitchen table, they pooled all of their recollections of a family vacation they took to Lake George, New York, when they were just children. Grasping a fading opportunity, the family shared some sweet laughter together before exhaustion hit, sending Billy back upstairs to lie down. Anna was making preparations to leave when the message was delivered, "Billy wants to see you." Anna breathed a thankful sigh as she began to climb the familiar stairs, making her way to her brother's room.

This room had always been his. It was never a very big room and it seemed even smaller with all of the paraphernalia necessary for his daily existence scattered about the room. Anna took note of a worn pair of shoes sitting beneath the bedside stand. A row of neckties hung neatly on pegs beside the closet door. A stack of good will in the form of recently received cards and letters lay on the dresser beside pictures of nieces and nephews, siblings and grandparents—family. Today it seemed a holy place, made sacred by the one who was working so hard to survive when survival seemed impossible.

Anna's eyes fell upon the ebbing form of the hero of the scene. She moved toward him, seated herself beside him on the bed, and began to rub the tired fleshless shoulders.

They spoke of old times, old friends, and familiar places. They spoke of the new friend Death that was lingering nearby, waiting to free him from the physical sufferings he had endured for so long. She compared the process of death to the process of birth—of moving through darkness, out of the body, and into the light of a new world. He spoke in terms that were unfamiliar to her and would later prove to be an invaluable clue to his understanding of existence and soul progression. He said he saw death as merely "moving to the next phase of life." The idea of being FINISHED with life and strolling leisurely about heaven didn't seem to suit him too well. "LIVE ON in Peace" seemed more appropriate to him than the traditional "REST in Peace." Anna's understanding of this came much later.

All too soon, it was time to go. She gave one last loving stroke to the weary shoulders and walked around the bed to where she could better see his face.

"Thanks for rubbing my back," he quietly said. "I don't get the chance for much physical contact anymore." The words cut deeply into Anna's unsuspecting heart. Why was it that the ones who needed the most touching, got the very least? Anna saw that she had unwittingly given her brother an invaluable gift that day—something uniquely hers to give, and it felt very good indeed.

As she started for the door, Billy stopped her and asked if she would do something for him—one last favor—a message to relay.

She approached the bed one more time. "Could you tell Karen for me," his soulful eyes met hers, "I don't think I will be at her wedding. I don't think I can hang on that long. She'll be disappointed. Break it to her gently."

Their youngest sister was engaged to be married and planned a springtime wedding. None of them had ever believed Billy would survive that long. Apparently, HE had—until that moment. Had he finally accepted his destiny?

With this final commission given, Anna started to leave. She consciously phrased her words—"I'll see you later." No real good-byes. Not yet. He asked her if she planned to stay the night, for the next day was a holiday—Labor Day—the milestone anniversary for Anna who had received news of his illness only a year earlier. She asked him if he wanted her to stay. She knew she couldn't—but she WOULD have if he had wished it.

"No..."

That was her cue. He was releasing her as she had only moments before released him. "You know you are free to move on anytime, Billy," she had said. "We'll be OK. You don't need to hang around here anymore. Whenever you're ready..." At that point, however, Anna mentally determined to see him one more time before he died, though she didn't know how or if that would be possible...

*   *   *

Anna was told on more than one occasion, that the grief she experienced at the eventual loss of her brother was an inordinate grief. The depth of sorrow and the intensity of the pain she experienced at his death were more appropriately felt at the loss of spouse or child. The deep bond that existed between the two of them was something that even she could not explain at first. Who was he that his death could leave her groping about in the darkness like a helpless child?

"Thank-you for watching out for me," was what she felt so strongly compelled to say to him that last time they talked. The words seemed barely adequate to express what she was feeling.

"What do you mean?" he asked her. Anna groped for an answer and finally cited an incident in college when he and his friends had conspired to lure her away from an unacceptable suitor. She refused the shrewd offer of a date by one noble volunteer. But when she eventually came to her senses and freed herself from the objectionable fellow, Billy and company had treated Anna to a celebration dinner.

The answer satisfied him, but what Anna felt as she gazed upon the one who had showed so much concern for her well-being along the way, was something far deeper and so obscured that she would not completely understand it until many seasons had passed. For what she did not realize at the time, was that locked up in the deep and hidden places of her being was the child she had once been. This child was an integral yet overlooked part of her. The loss of her brother—her inner child's childhood comrade and friend, the one who shared her secrets and had come to her aid, offering sweet comfort during difficult moments of childhood—would leave this little one screaming for recognition and consolation.

Eventually, Anna gained a fuller understanding of Billy's protective role in her past. These gradual revelations only brought with them a deeper and more profound sense of loss. Throughout the whole grief process, unfolding before her was the image of a little boy, a gangly youth, a young man who had believed in her—someone who had seen something in her that was worthy of respect, and who had risen to her defense on more than one occasion, expressing indignation and regret when no one else in Anna's world seemed to see or understand.

The grief Anna eventually felt at the loss of her brother was far from inordinate. She was losing an invaluable ally and a trusted friend—the one person in her life who unfailingly demonstrated that she had value and was worth protecting—her "bridge over troubled waters."

This knight in shining armor soon passed from the scene, leaving a terrible emptiness and pain. Anna groped for many long months before she began to realize that in the absence of her valiant protector, she was finally beginning to stand on her own. The long months of bitter soul agony bore the sweet fruit of peace. She emerged with her own sense of value, dignity, and self-respect. And found within herself the courage and the strength to be her own advocate and defender.

Perhaps this is what Billy wanted for her. Perhaps this is why he left her when she desperately wanted him to stay. Maybe he knew that the time had finally come for this baby bird to spread her own tiny wings—and fly.

CHAPTER SIX

▼

MOVING TO THE NEXT PHASE

"I know now that it is time for me to go, as i am slowly being drained of my life…therefore i shall thank whoever be responsible for the beauty and good that was brought into my life, and for what i have given to others surrounding me."
—bob goehring

A year had passed since Anna first became witness to her brother's long and courageous battle with AIDS. She had been given a rare privilege—a front row seat to a drama that was no doubt replaying itself a thousand different times in a thousand different places throughout the world. Through its many acts and countless scenes she had reluctantly held her seat, determined to see it through to the finish. And now the curtain was about to fall on her brother's young life and she would be left on her own to play the critic, write the reviews, and determine what it had all meant.

At her brother's bedside, a constant vigil was being kept. The tired body responded feebly to the loving ministrations of Anna's parents, and family members who lived nearby and lent their support. The blessed morphine Billy had insisted on earlier was delivering its soothing relief and he was no longer in pain. Friends and relatives alike were making last visits to the sickbed. Phone reports were called out to the waiting company of loved ones around the country. The world held its breath and they waited.

Time. She wanted it to stop. And yet she longed for it to finish its deadly mission. There was too much of it. And then there was not enough of it. It became friend and enemy rolled into one. Caught in its trap, Anna made her fumbling efforts to live. She moved mechanically through the dawdling days, very much aware that the next moment might bring the news she dreaded.

She had not forgotten her determination to speak with Billy one last time. It seemed an impossibility. But as she wandered through those endless days, with time everywhere and thoughts tumbling one upon the other, Anna began to understand what it was that still needed to be said.

As the days passed, she felt a growing urge—a growing responsibility—to make sure that Billy knew the truth about himself and his life. Society had done its best to cast him off as an unpleasant statistic. Religion had more than subtly implied that his life and its value were questionable. People in his situation had been written off on more than one occasion. She did not know how much of this he had taken to heart. It was inconceivable to her that he should die with even a trace of the shame or guilt or the humiliation the world might be pleased to see him carry with him into the grave.

"What a waste," some might say, looking at the dying form of the brilliant young man whose life had barely begun. For some reason, when the young died, people tended to think of their lives in terms of time and accomplishment. They would see years of education, potential, brilliance, and the hope of tomorrow snuffed out and laid to rest in a premature grave. Anna knew that Billy had fallen into such thinking himself years earlier, when a young friend's life had been cut short by the very virus that now consumed him. "What a waste," he had sadly remarked when passing the information along to her.

But there was so much more to a human life than what it knew, or what it did, or what it COULD do if it had the chance. A life WAS what it WAS, not what it MIGHT be someday. And no life that had brought such light and laughter to those around it could be simply tossed aside and considered "a waste." Anna wanted Billy to know just how valuable, how full and complete his life was—AS IS.

Anna was also plagued by the tragic thought that Billy's would probably be considered a "meaningless" death. After all, it didn't HAVE to happen this way. AIDS was the unfortunate consequence of some choices Billy didn't HAVE to make. Anna saw such reasoning as blind to the fact that all lives and all experiences, were the manifestation of 'consequence.' Some of these could be pleasant; some could bring pain; but both kinds could originate in moments of deep joy and celebration.

Anna remembered an incident that happened soon after the birth of her second son. The elation surrounding his arrival, and the early support and assistance of loving friends, began to dissipate with the establishment of their new daily routine. The sudden changes and the fatigue that comes with each new baby's arrival began to take their toll on her. Tears of frustration flowed easily and she longed for some kind soul to help her bear the load.

Dragging herself, her toddler, and her baby into the church nursery one drizzly Sunday morning, Anna gave voice to the difficulty she was experiencing, hoping to find some understanding or support in this hard adjustment. Her friend's reaction to her situation hurt for a long time and later gave her a clue to what her brother might have felt when his pain was similarly invalidated. Anna's friend broke insensitively into the well-known strains of a popular car commercial—"You asked for it, you got it."

Yes. She had asked for it. No. It didn't HAVE to happen this way. No one had made her want a second child. This was a choice she didn't HAVE to make. These were consequences she didn't HAVE to experience. But did this somehow disqualify her from kindness?

How easy it seemed to ignore people's sufferings, to resort to fault finding and blame, to excuse oneself from the work of compassion, and add to the pain of one's fellow man. How simple it would be to write off her brother's death as a senseless tragedy. Anna longed for one last chance to reassure him that there was meaning and significance to his life and passing.

As she waited through the long days preceding Billy's death, Anna also pondered the illusive idea of 'destiny.' It was a concept she had seldom considered. Its meaning had something to do with a person's purpose for being—why they were here—what they were meant to accomplish. With her limited understanding of such things, Anna began to reason that if Billy was dying of AIDS at the age of 38, then somehow this WAS his destiny.

It was not pleasant to see it that way. Her concept of his destiny had been that he should grow old with her and be there for her the whole way through. But there was obviously some reason for things happening this way or it wouldn't be so. Anna had barely begun to appreciate what Billy's full purpose might actually be, but she believed in it.

As the days and hours ticked slowly by, Anna's resolve solidified, her thoughts came together, and life graciously brought the two of them together in his final hour.

*　　　　　*　　　　　*

The last Sunday morning of a mild September dawned with a brilliant, clear sky. The sun was just taking the chill off of the early morning air when the unexpected sound of a ringing telephone pierced the morning quiet.

"You need to come home," her father's voice was filled with urgency on the other end of the line. "Your brother needs you." The message turned Anna's plans for a leisurely visit with Billy later that afternoon, into a desperate hope that she wouldn't get there too late.

She and her husband hastily made arrangements for the care of their children and before long they were on the road, making the two hour journey north, not knowing what they would find when they got there.

Anna was amazed at the workings of her mind—that it could KNOW the coming events were inevitable; and yet, because they were so unpleasant, it would try to reason those events away.

"Oh, it's just the weather that's giving him a hard time today," she tried to convince herself. "The extra humidity and lower air pressure would make breathing more difficult for anyone in his condition. Right?"

"This isn't the end—not yet!"

"I don't think he'll die until this evening—maybe after 7," she haphazardly predicted. She had even brought an overnight bag in case that happened.

Would they ever get there? She still needed to talk to him. Anna wasn't finished yet, not by a long shot. He just had to be OK long enough to hear that he didn't do anything wrong, that he was the most beautiful and courageous person she had ever known...

For two hours, they drove—first in silence, and then with agitated recitations of the muddled thoughts going through her head. For two hours, the weight of an unknown future hung heavily on her shoulders. There had been no preparation—no dress rehearsal—no script—nothing to tell them what they were all supposed to do next. She was just one of a ragged band of players, converging on the scene of their hero's final performance.

At last, the car came to its final stop. Anna threw open the door and rushed into the waiting arms of her parents and siblings. They all spoke at once, leading her up the stairs, filling her in on the sudden turn Billy had taken through the night and the rapid deterioration of his condition. They told her how they kept reassuring him that she would soon be there.

One more step—a turn of the corner—and she was again by his side, her wish fulfilled.

"I'm here, Billy," Anna said, placing a hand on his heaving shoulders. "I'm here. Are you going away now? Are you getting ready to leave us?"

Billy had been lying on his side, facing away from Anna's entry when she leaned over his shoulder and asked him the simple question. In truth, he had been comatose for hours. But with the posing of the question, the frail body revived and with Herculean effort, he turned ever so slightly in Anna's direction. His noble eyes fell upon hers and in a remarkably clear, strong voice, he uttered his final word.

"Yes…"

Anna added her encouragement to that of the others, telling him it was OK. They had released their claim on him. He was free to go.

After a moment Anna backed away and took in the incredible scene that lay before her. Billy had expressed his desire to die in his own bed, in his own room, surrounded by family. Weeks earlier, he had even arranged the bedroom furniture, making sure there would be space for each of them to be near him. How he had actually managed to accomplish his dream was beyond her understanding. She had been told many months earlier that people die when they choose to die—they die when they are ready. What Anna was now seeing suggested that this was indeed so.

Anna's mind soon fell to her one remaining task. This was not what she had envisioned as she had prepared herself for this small mission. She had planned to talk with her brother one on one, explaining herself to him as she went along. She had not expected an audience. She had not imagined he would be so incapable of responding to her.

She was troubled, knowing that time was incredibly short. There was no room for hesitation. She must say her peace now or never regain the chance. Her need to speak finally overrode her inhibitions and with her family bearing witness, Anna again leaned over the dying form, placed her hand upon his shoulder, and in an act of final benediction, poured out her heart and soul to him…

"Your life was not a waste, Billy—" (could he hear her? DID he hear her?)

"Your death has meaning—" Anna willed him to hear—and to KNOW...

"You have fulfilled your destiny."

        *   *   *

The 'time' which had hung so precariously over Anna's head during the past few weeks began to vanish. The curtain began to fall. She let her hand drop to her side and then stepped awkwardly away, her last duty performed.

With her brother's soul about to take its leave, Anna made her way to her younger brother's side, and leaned her head on his shoulder. "Sisters need their brothers," she said quietly, fighting the tears.

Together they waited...

It wasn't long.

Within a few moments, the incessant cough that had plagued Billy for more than a year, at last grew quiet—the labored breathing ceased—and the fevered brow began to cool.

Outside, a warm September sun shown brightly...

CHAPTER SEVEN

▼

BILLY'S "LAST HURRAH"

"Look at me sailing on the sea;
You'll only find my ship and me.
My sails are full against the sun.
I journey to the light of dawn.
Thinking of the time I've lost,
Weigh the price and pay the cost;
But high and dry the Albatross will fly..."
—*Chuck Moses*

All deaths are sudden.

It matters little that you have known for over a year that this was going to happen, that you have been watching and waiting for this moment to come, that you have in fact, arranged your whole life around it and the process leading up to it. The fact remains that one minute your loved one is with you, living and breathing and completely accessible, and the next minute he is not. This was Anna's conclusion. For nothing she had done to prepare herself for this inescapable moment had helped. Billy was gone. And his departure was as sudden as if the earth had opened and swallowed him up as he walked cheerfully down the street.

She couldn't remember what she had thought this moment would be like, or how she would react. What she DID know was that for the first time in all of the many months she had been dealing with her brother's situation, she felt herself to be completely and utterly alone—alone in her joy for him in accomplishing the incredible task of living; alone in her sense of awe over the miracle of death; alone in her personal sense of abandonment and longing to follow along through the veil that had opened to receive her brother's spirit. Such wonders. Such depths. And yet, the one she longed to share them with was now making his way into the hidden worlds and his new life on the other side.

Until this very moment, Anna had leaned heavily on Billy himself to get her through the dark times. He had been the rock, the center of focus, the one each of them could look to for affirmation that he was alive and well and "right here if you need me."

So many times she had called him or talked to him and drawn on his life and energy, making them her very own. Anna had survived thus far with his very essential help—help that was now very conspicuous in its absence. But no one is ever truly alone. When one source of comfort and support gives out, others are sure to take its place, as Anna was soon to find out.

                    *   *   *

Monday morning found a lost soul wandering hopelessly through the neighborhood mall, shopping for last minute accessories to her own little family's funeral wardrobe. She had overlooked these final details in all of the previous days' distractions. There was a certain insanity to what she was doing—wandering about, groping her way through the men's department, rummaging through ties and shirts. Everything here was 'Billy.' She passed the men's cologne counter. 'Billy' again.

She passed the bookstore. Billy had worked with books. He worked in publishing. He had always planned to write a book someday—an historical novel about a small Southern town at the turn of the century—the town to which their family traced its paternal roots. Would he ever write it, she wondered?

No...

No, that would never be, now. Remember? Anna remembered, and the previous day's events came crashing in on her again with a newer and deeper severity. She walked on.

Anna soon found herself staring blankly into the shop where she usually went to have her hair trimmed. "I should probably go in there," she thought. It had been months now since she first began coaxing her hair to a longer length. The remnants of the old style had left her hair looking a bit ragged. "I should go in there. But I don't really want to see anyone. I don't really want to talk to anyone. What if I break down? What if I prattle on like a fool?"

Hesitantly, she approached the desk, and from a very safe place deep inside herself, she watched as she gave them her name and told them why she was there. Anna watched as she was led through a maze of chairs and mirrors to a place near the far wall.

"What can I do for you today?" asked the young man standing beside her. His name was Jeffrey. Anna had seen him in the shop a few times before. The most notable quality she had seen him display was his good humor and penchant for fun—a humor that couldn't quite hide a deeper and more sensitive side. It was no mistake that she should find herself sitting here at this particular moment on this particular day.

As Jeffrey worked some magic with his scissors and comb, he simultaneously began to work a miracle with Anna—the miracle of unsolicited friendship and support for a basic stranger. From the safety of her chair she DID break down. She prattled on like a fool. And though the young man didn't have to listen, he listened. Though he didn't have to ask how she was holding up, he asked...and he cared.

Jeffrey gave Anna a great gift that afternoon; and yet, she felt like she offered him little in return. In fact, she felt like she had little to offer anyone in her present condition. This was all very new to her, and she found herself wondering—had her brother felt this way, so utterly needy with no real resources to draw on—so little to give? Did he have to fight with himself in order to let himself be taken care of, knowing he could never repay the favor? Anna felt that pain—the ego wound—the deep longing to stand on one's own again and let all of the comforters go home. But it was not to be—not for Billy; nor, during this short interlude, for Anna.

There was little more she could do than abandon herself to the ministrations of this young stranger, and let the tears of gratitude as well as grief flow as he took her hand in his and said, "It's all right. He's in good hands where he is."

Anna walked away from her new friend that day with a lighter burden and a renewed sense that there was something right in the world. People still cared.

*   *   *

Anna's family set the next two days aside for the observance of calling hours and the funeral. Billy's influence was strongly felt as the last wishes he so carefully prepared and recorded in earlier, healthier days were faithfully carried out. To the finest detail, Billy seemed to order the atmosphere and the events that would see him to his final resting place. From the color of the shirt he wanted to wear to the final engraving on his headstone—it was all written down. No need to think. No need to decide. He had done it all for them. That—and more. For far beyond the physical details one could visibly see, with nary a word of instruction, Billy had unwittingly or perhaps deliberately set the stage for the ultimate healing of them all.

As Anna's family gathered from far and near, three young men in New York City packed their bags preparing for a long journey west. Their friend and colleague had passed away on Sunday afternoon and they had each been given a great honor. According to their friend's wishes, they had each been called upon to serve as pallbearer.

Across a long Tuesday, they made their way to their friend's home town. They found a room, then settled in to rest awhile before the evening calling hours.

At the small country funeral home across town, neighbors and friends of the bereaved gathered to pay their last respects and offer their condolences and support. One by one they came. One by one they shook the extended hands offered by the family and said "I'm so sorry." One by one they walked on.

Once again, out on the highway, three young men made their way toward the their departed friend's side. This time, they were nervous. Uncomfortable. They were aware they were walking onto potentially hostile ground. They knew Billy. They knew how he had suffered silently trying to avoid the harsh judgment of his family's religion. They expected no more than little regard to be held toward them. They hoped all could remain civil if not friendly. Who knew?

Their speed slowed. Three times they stopped to gather their nerve, unsure of themselves—unsure of how this family would receive them. They didn't need approval, but could they simply be accepted? Three times they resumed the last leg of their journey to take up the task they had agreed to perform. Three times they let their love and loyalty to their friend overrule any last minute apprehensions.

At the funeral home, time ticked slowly by as Anna's family continued to receive guests. She had picked up somewhere in the haze of the last few days' events that some of her brother's friends were coming in from New York. It seemed like a far away detail, but she half watched the crowd for the unfamiliar faces. More hands to shake. More comfort to give, with the evening half over. Finally, in the shadow of the entryway, the door opened and three young men stepped inside, hoping to slip quietly to the back sitting area, eluding detection for a little while. How nice it would have been to hide out and regather their strength. But the clocks around the world had finally struck the hour when past wrongs would be righted.

As it became known to Anna's family that "the guys" had finally arrived, the miracle occurred. One by one family members left their duties to the public. Each of them rushed toward the door where her brother's friends waited. Smiles broke out on all faces. Hugs. Then tears. With unexpected tenderness, Anna's family drew the young men into the room, stopping before the place where her brother's body lay. And there among the bronze mums and yellow roses that draped her brother's casket, Billy's two worlds became one.

Time stood still as family and friends finally embraced each other, melding the significant people in Billy's life into a single continuous whole. Anna watched spellbound. Like long lost relatives reunited after ages of exile in separate hostile lands they came together. There was Glen, the 'laundry man' from that cold wintry week of testing back in February. Once a stranger, he would soon become her vital and precious friend. Then Doug, his gentle and supportive companion. And finally, Mitch—the "my friend Mitch" who was about to find out how he had rescued Anna when he rescued Billy that day not so long ago.

Billy's life was no longer fragmented. In death he was able to accomplish what had eluded him in life. The light of their common love for him drove the shadow of fear away and they all stepped out of their respective 'closets,' united in grief, connected by love, and one in heart. Anna was sure Billy smiled at the sight. She was certain he rested easier knowing that they now had each other to help share the burden he had placed on them with his early departure. They would add new names to old address books. Their phone bills would reflect growing friendships and concerns. And life would go on with a broader and deeper base of encouragement and support.

It was not necessarily the rule. In time Anna became aware that many families who were dealing with AIDS often isolated themselves from their loved one's life and friends and lovers. They were unable to accept the realities of that loved one's life. But separation could only add pain to pain. Perhaps it is all they were capable of, but there was such a 'missing out' and an opportunity for healing that could never be replaced—the healing of all parties involved.

Walls would have served no useful purpose in their situation now. Indeed, they never had. Anna could not fathom how she would have been able to recover from her devastating loss without frequently accessing the bridges that now connected her to her brother's friends—ANNA's friends. The plain and simple truth?—they needed each other.

The final events surrounding Billy's funeral began to whiz by. The party took on an almost festive air as they all tried to say everything and then hear everything the others had to say. They laughed and they cried. They held onto each other, dreading the thought of more good-byes. They did their best to make up the lost years. They filled in the missing pieces for each other and decided that in losing one family member, they had each gained many more.

*　　　　　　*　　　　　　*

Wednesday morning dawned with a weeping sky and a slight chill in the air. The newly bonded group converged on the funeral home one last time and focused their thoughts on the life that had recently passed from them. Readings were read. Songs were sung. Prayers were prayed. And a coffin, born solemnly by a curious mix of newfound friends was carried to its final place of rest.

In the early evening, in a final ceremonial act, they returned to the graveside to say their last good-byes. Their numbers had dwindled throughout the afternoon as different ones returned to life and its varied responsibilities. But those of them who remained were soon tumbling out of a half dozen cars and gathering around the lone patch of sacred ground.

Anna stood silently, with her own private thoughts. It had been a wondrous day. The chattering died down. And then they began to sing. It was a tradition of Anna's family to close each of its significant gatherings by honoring its Southern heritage. How fitting to remember to do this for the one, who for all of the difficulties along the way, loved his family more deeply than them all. Minus one distinctive tenor voice, they sang the familiar strains of "Dixie." As they continued to sing, their hearts lightened and their grave side visit became a celebration of life as the clouds suddenly parted revealing a glorious golden sunset.

"That's Billy," Anna's uncle confidently remarked.

And so it was.

The sun's rays bathed their foreheads, christening each of them with its golden light, sharing its unmistakable message of hope.

"You must carry on," it said. "Keep living."

"Remember me alive, for I am alive. Do not weep for me, for I am not dead. Keep laughing! Smile! Enjoy!"

"I have finished."

"You must still run."

"I will cheer you on!"

The message of Life that Anna had seen radiating from her brother's being, during those first few months of knowing this day would eventually come, remained. "Life is still 'today.' It belongs to us all equally. Use it wisely. Use it well."

The sun soon set, scattering the small band of friends back into the world from which they had come. Life would go on. But a small touch from their friend and loved one would go with them. They might not see, but it would be there. And they would all take with them the memory of a time and place when heaven came to earth, kissed their cheek, and blessed them with its life-giving words...

"...Carry on!"

PART TWO

▼

THE FIRST YEAR

CHAPTER EIGHT

▼

"DID ANYONE THINK OF TOM TODAY?"

In the darkness I pray for some light
To fall down from the heavens tonight.
Curing all, its benevolent rays;
I write this song for the oncoming day,
When the fighting is over,
And the children come home...
—Chuck Moses

Morning dawned on the day following Billy's funeral. It dawned just as it always had. Anna was not sure how or why it happened, but it did. And with that dawning, life began to move again, luring her away from the place of final good-byes.

She did not go willingly. She wanted to stay in the soft dark bed of grief with the covers drawn over her head for as long as she could. Who needed life? Her brother was gone.

Anna spent a few days holding desperately onto the old, before life's strong currents were able to loosen her grip and carry her to her next stop. There was much left for her to see, though she felt she had seen enough. There were priceless treasures buried in the pain she was feeling. Robert Browning's words seemed appropriate—"A whole I planned; youth shows but half. Trust God, see all, nor be afraid."

Anna began to realize that she needed to pick herself up out of her grief and rejoin the land of the living. Billy had made a list of people he knew and cared about—people who would need to know that he had moved on. Anna agreed to call several on the list that she knew.

It was not an easy task, dialing old friends and acquaintances and reviewing the week's events over and over again. But it needed to be done. Anna found herself in the ironic position of comforting people as they realized their loss. She listened as distraught voices told her what her brother had meant to them over the years.

During one call, the wife of one of his older friends picked up a tiny silver cup that Billy had given their oldest son when he was born. "He was his godfather, you know?" No. Anna didn't know…until then. Later that night Anna received a call from the woman's husband who was in London on business. In tears, he related how Billy served as Best Man at his wedding. "I couldn't have gotten married without him," he said.

Anna was repeatedly showered with expressions of love and appreciation for her brother and all he had done for his friends. They painted for her a striking portrait of their very well loved and admired friend. They would feel the loss.

With her mind out and about, connecting with people Anna had not thought of for years in some cases, her thoughts went back to a three-way phone conversation she and Billy had had with an old college friend of theirs named Tom. That was back in the days when AIDS belonged to other people and they were free to speak of it with less emotion and concern.

Tom had called Billy, hoping to discount a rumor that a mutual acquaintance had been lost to AIDS. The rumor was proved to be just that—a rumor. But the occasion had given way to a lot of playful verbal bantering and remembering of old times.

Tom was at the party Anna threw in honor of Billy's 21st birthday, the year they were all in Bible college together. He was a good listener as both of them adjusted to college life. They were freshmen together. At one point, Tom felt comfortable enough to confide in Anna his concern about his sexual orientation. It was a source of constant struggle and guilt. He had hoped to receive some helpful guidance from the college counseling staff. But instead, one day he wandered to the steps of the dorm she lived in and informed her that the administration had just kicked him out of school because of it.

Anna cried for him the day he left, and she had never forgotten how cruel and senseless it all seemed. She didn't suppose Tom found such harsh rejection and disregard to be very helpful either. They eventually lost touch, though Anna occasionally heard of his path crossing with Billy's in New York.

A picture of Tom was growing strong and clear in Anna's mind. Was his name on someone else's list? Had he been overlooked? She called home to check, but his name did not turn up anywhere. So she decided to dive in and make some calls of her own. She had to locate him. She knew he would want to know that Billy was gone.

The last number she had for him was in Chicago. When that turned out to be a dead end, Anna checked directory assistance. No luck. She decided that she would have the most success if she located Tom's sister. She would probably still be at the address listed in the college directory. Anna dialed the number and waited.

The phone rang once.

It rang again.

"Hello." It was Beth.

"Hi, I am trying to get in touch with your brother Tom. Do you have his current phone number or some way I could contact him?" Anna came straight to the point of her call.

Beth seemed distracted for a moment—maybe even a bit confused. Finally, she asked, "Who is this?"

Anna told her.

Silence.

When Beth slowly began to speak again, Anna found herself slipping into a new sadness.

"I'm sorry," she sighed. "Tom passed away three years ago. I guess you didn't know."

This time, Anna was distracted. "What took him?" She asked…knowing.

"AIDS," was Beth's answer.

What followed was an awkward exchange of distressing information that miraculously transformed itself into a soothing balm for both of them. Like Anna, Beth had been left behind. Both of them had a part of themselves they could no longer express, because the ones who were meant to receive those expressions were gone. That Tom had been gone almost three years and Billy, little more than three days, made no difference. Beth understood. Anna understood. And in THAT lay the comfort they both needed at the time.

In the course of their conversation, Anna learned that the inner struggle Tom had been dealing with in those early days at college had never left him. Tom had never really been able to make peace with his gayness. In his understanding, his church and his God could not accept this in him. Tom had been torn between these two forces, trying to please his God and then falling honestly yet miserably back into the gay lifestyle. At last he had given up and moved to San Francisco. There he surrounded himself with friends and a church that would be understanding of his life as it was. There he received a disconcerting diagnosis. There he developed AIDS-related lymphoma. And there he died and his ashes would be kept in honor of his beautiful young life.

As Beth finished the record of the short life of this wonderful human being who had been her friend, Anna felt his pain. She did not know how he had been able to endure such ongoing inner turmoil. He was a tortured soul. And sadly, she realized it had not been much different for her own brother.

She had no answers for such a dilemma. Somehow, somewhere there had to be a peaceful place where all persons could find acceptance in all of life's conditions. It had to make sense. The kind of pain that Tom and a thousand others seemed so obligated to bear, HAD to serve some useful purpose or it had to be eliminated. Tom's story only served to fuel the fires within her to make her own peace with her brother's adopted lifestyle. Someday she would understand.

As her conversation with Tom's sister began to come to a close, Beth asked expectantly, "Were you thinking of Tom yesterday?"

Anna remembered the strong vision of Tom's face that had haunted her over the past few days. "I've been thinking of him all week," she said in reply.

"I just wondered," she said, reflecting on Anna's answer, "because yesterday was Tom's birthday. And I was wondering as the day was going by, 'Is anyone in the whole world thinking of my brother today?' I just always wonder about it."

"My dear friend Tom," Anna laughingly thought. "You found a way to help us both today." She pictured him winking in delight. In fact, she suddenly imagined him standing there with his arm thrown over her own brother's shoulder, and both of them smiling and agreeing, "Those girls needed each other today." Then she pictured them shaking hands—mission accomplished—and buzzing about the heavens on some other jovial mission.

Through that single phone call, Anna began to realize that she was not alone in her grief. It marked the beginning of the connections she was going to be making with others in her situation. And it heightened her awareness of the fact that she was being tenderly cared for by forces beyond the physical world.

Surely it was not mere coincidence that Anna's heart could long for an understanding ear and that such a person should enter her life within hours. Nor was it mere coincidence that Beth should scan the world, in search of someone who remembered her precious brother, and that such a "someone" should call her, asking about his welfare the very next afternoon. Eventually, she began to lose her total surprise when the perfect situation would suddenly materialize before her, providing her with the comfort or confidence she needed to move to the next step.

Anna also came to understand that day, that her life, freshly wounded as it was, could somehow be utilized to help ease the burdens of another. She was beginning to find some hope. Perhaps, she would one day look back and say it had been worth it.

Anna was not to be finished with Tom so easily. Months later, as she was rocking absently in her favorite rocking chair, with sleeping babe nestled deep in her arms, Anna was suddenly overcome with the presence of her old friend. It was as if he were there in the room with her, dancing in the evening shadows. He was very excited and seemed eager to relay some important message.

"What is it?" Anna asked—out loud, as much as within. Tom's playful energy swirled around her. An unanticipated giggle escaped her lips as she went on, "I AM listening! What do you need to say?"

"I'm HOME!"—was his emphatic reply.

"And I'm FREE!" She sensed his enthusiasm.

"TELL THEM!"

This dear soul—so troubled he had been, trying to mesh the reality of his homosexuality with the teachings of the church he so respected and loved. The struggle was over. He had found the place of unconditional acceptance—indeed he had never truly left it—and he was now at peace. He thought for some reason that she might be able to share his message with the world. Anna promised him that quiet winter evening that if she ever found a way, she would "TELL THEM"...and the world WOULD know.

This chapter is lovingly
dedicated to the memory of
Tom
HOME—FREE

CHAPTER NINE

▼

LIGHT FROM THE OTHER SIDE

"Where there is true love, there is no separation."
—*White Eagle*

A scene from Charles Dickens' A Christmas Carol kept going through Anna's head as she moved into late October. It was a scene near the end of the story in which a reluctant Ebenezer Scrooge is being escorted through the future by the dark and wordless Ghost of Christmas Yet to Come. He is taken to a dingy, disreputable side of town where bundles of his belonging are being heartlessly pawned and traded, he being recently deceased.

Though her family's present mission was vastly different in intent and tone, the scene remained fixed in Anna's mind. With what would have been Billy's 39th birthday barely past, and with Billy himself so freshly removed from them, the unpleasant but just as unavoidable task of dispersing his belongings needed to be done.

Anna did not play an active role in the proceedings, but she knew what was happening, and she was aware of the kind of pain it was bringing to other members of her family. It was another step in closing a chapter in their lives that none of them wanted to leave yet.

The few meager possessions that had once been her brother's and were about to become hers, arrived via moving van on a rainy fall evening. The various boxes and bags were unloaded and placed about on her living room floor. They constituted a humbling memorial to a life that had once been.

It was just stuff. And yet those few items that had once brought comfort and convenience to her brother only served to magnify the great gulf that now separated them. He had passed from the material world she felt so locked into. He had no use for blankets or towels or lamps—or bothersome sisters, for that matter. He was in heaven. How convenient...for HIM.

She knew that the idea of heaven was meant to be a comfort. For some it was, no doubt. But for Anna it had become a hostile place. It had ruthlessly snatched her brother into its blissful realms and seemed to think that this should make her happy. She would see him again someday, she had been told—someday after she had turned ninety-five and muddled her way through life with only fading memories of her brother—her friend. She would then pass through the gates of death and be reunited with him. Maybe, with a little luck, she would recognize him and he would remember who she was.

"The separation is only for a season. It won't last forever," she had also heard. But even the first few weeks had seemed too long. She missed him. She missed him so much, and all the glories of his heaven did little to ease the emptiness and utter loneliness she felt for him. If only she could see him one more time. If only they could talk. If only he would pick up the phone and call. But no. He was in heaven and there she was, alone late at night, sitting among the boxes and bags, wondering about stuff, and heaven, and feeling totally cut off from someone she still needed desperately to love.

Anna stood to her feet, surveying the scene one last time, and then headed over to turn off one of the newly arrived living room lamps. It was late and sleep beckoned to her. The soft glow from beneath the shade drew her into its circle of warmth. Anna stood there waiting, though she didn't know why. Then, in a brief moment, this lamp that had faithfully cast its light upon her brother's life for more than a decade, suddenly became the embodiment of the one that she was missing so. With little thought for how silly it might seem, Anna laid her head upon the shade, wrapped her arms around its base, and began to cry.

Anna had already discovered that there was little use in burying this kind of pain. She knew it wouldn't go anywhere until she paid attention to it and let it have its say. And so she opened her heart and allowed this latest wave of grief to pour its cleansing waters over her wounds.

What happened in the next few moments was totally unexpected, yet altogether wondrous at the same time. Some would call it a miracle. To Anna it was the shining rainbow that follows a spring storm. In the depths of that quiet moment, as she stood there tearfully embracing a simple household lamp, Anna's brother came to her.

She did not see spirits, or feel any mysterious breezes. The lights didn't flicker or turn themselves off. Put very simply, she heard a voice. It was quiet, yet filled with strength, and there was no mistaking who it belonged to.

"I will shine a Light for you," the clear, loving voice of her brother's spirit promised.

The words came like a welcome rainstorm to a dry parched land. Anna absorbed their sound and their significance. She knew instinctively that the power that flowed within them would change the landscape of her inner world forever. She slipped to the floor and enfolded herself in her own arms. There she gently rocked, then her body shook, this time with joyful sobs as she realized she had not been forgotten. Billy was aware of her pain and had found a way to pierce the veil between them.

For all of her religious training to the contrary, it was not so surprising. Hadn't she seen that unquenchable flame of Life within him grow and intensify as his body deteriorated with sickness? What was happening that night was a mere extension of that dynamic: Life—indomitable Life. And it came with a purpose in mind. It came to share itself, bringing light into Anna's dark and hopeless world. Anna knew that a person like her was supposed to have all the answers. She was a Bible college student, graduated with honors. She had studied and taught the Scripture from its original languages. She was constantly analyzing and restructuring her faith in an effort to distill it into its purest form. She seemed driven by this near pathological need to please the holy, yet wrathful God of her childhood. It was an endless, exhausting task that now contributed little to her sense of well being.

With her brother's devastating diagnosis, lingering illness, and death, Anna had come at last to the end of her spiritual resources. The words were empty. The rituals—meaningless. The God—too cruel and distant to bother with anymore. With the onset of this impenetrable grief, the faith Anna had frantically tried to arrange in some suitable order ever since it all came crashing down so many months earlier, was all but dead in her. It had betrayed her in her greatest time of need and she was lost. She had no answers. She had nothing at all. And yet she had everything.

Into this dark and lonely place, Anna's brother came with a welcome promise of Light. It gave her new hope. She began to believe she might someday find her way through the spiritual maze she was lost in, and enter into the peace she longed for. But she would take a new path, forged through new and often forbidden territory, and her brother—the only spirit-being she was now capable of trusting—would be her guide.

Anna went to bed that night knowing that he was not so far away, that he would return to her, and would share with her something of the truth and light he had found on the other side. She was ready to learn. She had little to lose. With a great sense of relief, Anna released the old ways, the old God, the old beliefs that had tied her up in spiritual knots for so many years, while offering so little comfort and support in return. She laid her head on her pillow, exhausted, yet somehow knowing that the world was as it should be. Then curling up in the security of her brother's spirit-arms, she fell asleep.

The reconstruction phase of Anna's spiritual journey began almost immediately as three important books finagled their way into her life. A few days after receiving her brother's message, Anna's husband gave her a copy of Dr. Raymond Moody's classic study of the near-death experience, *Life After Life*. Brian had discovered the worn, coffee-stained volume hidden beneath the floorboards of an attic he was remodeling. He brought it home to Anna, thinking it might help.

Soon after that, during a visit home, she came across two paperbacks while sorting through her brother's books. *We Don't Die*, and *We Are Not Forgotten*, both by Joel Martin and Patricia Romanowski, had been sent to Billy by a friend and fellow AIDS patient named Gregory, soon after Billy moved home. These books expounded the work of psychic medium George Anderson, and recorded many conversations and loving messages he had received from souls on the other side of death's veil.

With her new teachers in book form, delivered safely into her possession, Anna unwittingly embarked upon the great adventure of spiritual discovery that life, up to this point, had graciously prepared her for.

As she began to read, the world that her brother had entered when he left her that day began to unfold and spread out before her in all of its beauty and wonder. Not a stark impersonal heaven. Not an inaccessible fortress only the dead were permitted to enter. But a vibrant, pulsating existence that fairly burst with love and acceptance—a place she was welcome to see and experience even then.

Through the eyes of the authors Anna took in the sights and sounds of the place she was beginning to think of as Home. The menacing God of her childhood was nowhere to be found. There were no creeds or dogmas, no shrines or churches, no hell. Only gentleness, understanding, and peace.

As she gazed around her, Anna was struck with the thought that life as she knew it, with all of its pain and problems, its joys and sorrows—the all-consuming struggle to find true and lasting happiness—was but a single stop, a temporary layover, on the long journey of soul progression. Birth had brought her into this existence. Death would send her on the continuing leg of her journey. But the Life and Being that she WAS, was eternal, indestructible, and sure of its destination. No wonder Billy had felt so casual about his approaching death. It was merely the next step for him. Or as he put it, "moving to the next phase of life."

Anna learned, that from their elevated vantage point above and beyond our limited existence, souls who had passed into the next stage through death were sending back this message of hope concerning man's earthly sojourn....We are here to learn. We are here to love. It is here, midst the fiery storms of this brief lifetime that souls have the opportunity to grow in understanding, wisdom, and love. Upward through the darkened surroundings, souls reach for the Sun and when they finally emerge, they blossom forth into all they were meant to be. There are no mistakes. It is all for a Purpose. Soul growth. Soul growth for all.

Our loved ones are alive. Our loved ones are aware of us and our sufferings, and they are ready to assist us if we will let them.

Anna sensed her brother's upholding presence many times throughout the months following his initial visit. She met him in her dreams. Sometimes in the midst of a busy day, a sudden warmth would hit her cheek. "A kiss from Billy," she would think, smiling. His love was hidden in the music she heard. Songs became messengers of assurance that he was there for her when she needed him. Anna found herself lighting candles for him and sending him mental telegrams. She even teased that he was becoming a nuisance. She reveled in the fact that Love was not limited by time or space, and she freely sent him huge daily doses of it. And all the while, Anna healed.

It would be wrong to give the impression that everything was always cozy and fine. It was not. When the sentiment she felt about his whole situation naturally dissolved into long days of bitter musings and angry accusation, Anna took a sadistic pleasure in knowing that Billy was right there, taking every punch of the verbal bashing she was sending his direction. "Was it worth it? Were a few moments of pleasure worth the horrendous agony you have put us all through?"

To his eternal credit, she never sensed her brother recoiling at any of her harsh judgments. If anything, Anna felt a strong sense of yearning—almost a pity, as if he longed for her to understand: "Oh, if only you could see what I see. And know what I know. You are gaining ever so much more than you have ever lost."

She could not stay angry. It was pretty hard to hold a grudge against someone who was drenching you with love and good will. But she never regretted those dark days either. Grief must show all of its faces before it is free to move on.

He promised her Light. And Anna believed he kept that promise. In all of her dark days of wandering about in the shadowy place of death, Billy remained firmly by her side, carrying the undying lantern of encouragement and hope.

It took Ebenezer Scrooge only one night and visits by three spirit beings to realize that life was more than material values and possessions. Rather, it is made up of sweet intangibles like friendship, laughter, and love. These are the things that endure.

Anna was not so sure but that in the grand scheme of the Universe, this may have been her brother's ultimate purpose—to shift her focus beyond the things that do not last and to awaken within her a life-changing awareness of the eternal. He had succeeded.

Anna often reflected on the path she trod, and she rejoiced with Mr. Scrooge that "the sprits [had] done it all in one night. They can do whatever they like. Of course they can. Of course they can." In Anna's case, it was many long nights, with innumerable lonely days thrown in, but the outcome was the same. She had awakened to a grand celebration, fully alive for the first time, and she would never be the same. Old Ebenezer Scrooge would have been pleased.

For Gregory
Thanks for the books!

CHAPTER TEN

▼

WHAT FRIENDS ARE FOR

"See to it now that you spend...more time
on finding the people you belong to."
—*Clarissa Pinkola Estes*

Old newspapers can lie around for weeks when there is nothing you need from them. But the one Anna was frantically searching for that late November day was long gone. She had glanced over it quickly a few days earlier and now her mind was unsuccessfully probing for some information she had seen in it. Someone in her hometown had pieced together an AIDS Memorial Quilt. Somewhere at sometime over the next few days, that quilt would be on display. But where? And when?

Anna did not believe that her deepest longing was to see the quilt, though she was curious about it. But its very existence indicated to her that there were others nearby who had been lost to this disease. And if that were the case, she was not the only one around who was trying to get through a difficult time. Not only that, but it also meant that the surviving loved ones had cooperated in the creation of this tribute. These were the flesh and blood people with whom she was feeling a growing desire to connect. It was more than a desire, it was a need—a need which was growing in intensity every day.

Anna's recent spirit ventures into Billy's world had brought peace to her at a very deep level. And yet, the physical, emotional, and practical earthly realities of loss were still very much a part of her. There was too much going on in her head to manage alone. There were too many angles she was trying to figure out. There was still a great deal of pain—too much to manage without the loving assistance of somebody in this world who KNEW first-hand what she was dealing with.

This is what she hoped to find when she sought out the AIDS quilt. She strongly suspected that if she could find this quilt, there would be some knowing soul standing beside it whom she could approach with her pain, feeling comfortable enough to share it with them.

The newspaper was gone. She had no phone number to call. She knew of no one in Cason whom she could ask for the information. But she had a plan. Venturing out that next weekend—the most likely time of the quilt's display, Anna systematically searched the local malls and business areas for any sign of it.

A beautifully handcrafted quilt hung on display in one store window. It was being raffled by a local women's group. A growing despair took over as she approached it, admiring the craftsmanship, yet realizing it was not what she was looking for. The evening ended and she gave up the search. She returned home empty-handed and alone.

Anna did not realize it at the time, but the Universe was aware of her need. And it was busily shuffling itself about, guaranteeing that she would soon connect with one, and then many, who would lovingly take her in and help her to pass safely through the fire.

For eight more weeks she traveled alone. Then a chance conversation with an acquaintance at the local library produced the long-awaited name and phone number of one of the most important AIDS support persons Anna would meet.

Her name was Joy.

Over the next few months, Anna came to see her as a woman of great courage and compassion. AIDS had claimed the life of her oldest son the year before she met her. But Joy had refused to give in to the general expectation that she quietly drift away, bearing her burden in stoical silence. Rather, the whole experience had inspired her to devote her time and energy toward making people aware of the reality of AIDS in the local community, and seeing that AIDS patients and their families were properly acknowledged and supported in their time of need.

Joy saw things as they truly were, and she was unfailingly, painfully honest when she talked about the issues. Anna got the feeling that if there was any insincerity lurking about within her, Joy would spot it in a minute and immediately call her on it. She never did that though, and Anna realized there was no need to fear. She was her friend. A fellow traveler on a difficult path; some of the most refreshing company she would encounter on her AIDS journey.

In the months that followed their initial phone meeting, Anna and Joy had many opportunities to talk. Through her vivid recollections Anna came to know and admire her son Nathan, who had last given his energetic service as stage manager for the Los Angeles area's rendition of *Phantom of the Opera*. Anna, too, was more than pleased to tell her about Billy's life and accomplishments. They were two wonderfully talented young men whose lives had been cut tragically short. The two women were mourning their loss, making their way through the grief process. But something in the bigger picture was drastically amiss. It didn't take much observation or experience to eventually put a finger on the pulse of the problem.

Clues were abundant. Like the day that Joy told Anna about a mother whose son had died of AIDS two years earlier. She told her that this mom had never told anyone how her son had actually died. It was her secret. No one was to know. Then there were others who refused to have patches placed in the local AIDS quilt for fear of being identified. Also, the obituary page of the local paper often printed the names of young men who "died after an extended illness," their families often requesting that donations be made to local libraries or cancer societies or places designed to mislead the casual reader.

Over the years, Anna would know of only one young man whose family unashamedly printed his cause of death in the paper—"died of AIDS." He was the fortunate son of a minister who dared to learn Love from a gay son. Anna also heard of some, who asked that memorial contributions be made to local hospice groups or organizations that were known to care for AIDS parents, but this was rare.

She believed there was more to this masking of circumstances than the issue of privacy. These were mere symptoms of a deeper, more troublesome problem.

She could see it. Death by AIDS was not the same as death by other causes. Anna understood that all too well now. When loved ones died by this most stigmatized of all diseases, families often took on the socially imposed shame and the stern judgment of the community around them. They suffered together. They experienced in miniature what their loved ones had experienced, in some cases, for a lifetime—suspicion, disregard, and the smug satisfaction that they were receiving their "just desserts." And the family's response was amazingly similar to theirs. They became afraid. They would hide. They would bury their heads in the sand, hoping no one would notice that they had loved and lost and grieved for the "least" of all human beings—gay persons with AIDS.

It wasn't like this for everyone. Joy was not the only mom who was out and loud and proud of her son. Thankfully people DID opt to openly love and support AIDS patients no matter what the mood of society might be. But without exception, people in Anna's position were all dealing with society's ignorance, insensitivity, and lack of support. People did not trip over themselves trying to find out how the bereaved were doing. There was not a long line of people waiting to help them or listen to them express the soul agony that losing a child or a sibling or a spouse had produced.

Apart from initial condolences, it took over two years for some of Anna's own in-laws to finally ask her how she was coping. By then the worst was over. Perhaps they sensed this with relief, and knew their questions would bear simple fruit, requiring little risk or effort on their part. But that was the point. These families were isolated. Isolated by society's fear of them and by their own fear of society. It was a double grief, a lonely grief, and everyone lost.

    *   *   *

One could only wonder if the lady at the post office felt she had lost a thing when she offered Anna moral crumbs at a time when she was still in need of continual soul sustenance. But she did. It was late in the year and months into her friendship with Joy and countless others just like her who she eventually met along the way. But she was still far from healed. That year, the U.S. Postal Service took a courageous step in issuing an "AIDS Awareness" stamp. It had a simple yet powerful design—red ribbon on white, with a black border. And for someone who was always looking for external support, its existence was very affirming.

Anna wanted some of those stamps. Actually, she wanted a lot of them. She wanted to always have the option of honoring Billy in this way.

So Anna wandered into a local gift shop one day, made her way to the mail desk in the back corner, and asked for a small quantity of this stamp. Apparently, she made a mistake or something. For certain, Anna let herself forget the fact that for many people, the subject of AIDS was still a loaded gun waiting to go off.

"I don't HAVE any of those stamps," snapped the woman behind the counter. "In fact, I sent those stamps back to the main office the other day. NOBODY wants to buy any of THOSE stamps." Nobody? But what about HER. Anna was stunned. Here she was, facing a dragon, and she was precariously alone and unarmed.

Anna finally recovered from this unexpected blast well enough to speak. She weakly stated, "But they say that before long everyone will know somebody who is dealing with AIDS."

She had apparently crossed the line. She had disturbed the slumbering beast and was soon caught in a verbal tirade about "immorality," and "the Bible says," and "if they would just listen," and "it's their own fault." On and on she went. Anna said nothing more, but dropped the electric bill into the mail slot and escaped the lair in as inconspicuous a manner as she could manage.

When she reached her car, she let the full weight of the incident crash in on her. She started to drown in the backwash. "Who does she think she is to spit on my brother's grave like that?" She was not angry so much as she was crushed by the woman's cruel disregard for her fellow human beings in need, and by her careless assumption that Anna would not mind the awful stinging of her words. She was so wrong about that.

It was Joy who rescued Anna. She was always rescuing people. Anna blessed her for it. Her friend's courage was contagious. She wore it close to her side, strapped to her very being like the mythical Excalibur.

Anna called her when she got home. Joy welcomed her with open arms and listened to her story with the righteous indignation Anna had expected. With her affirming words she picked Anna up and dusted her off and she began to relax once more. Anna breathed easier as she remembered something she had forgotten in the midst of the fray. She was not alone. There was a whole army of wonderful, caring people in the world who would gladly stand with her in a similar challenge.

Joy reminded her that they could not expect everyone to be there for them. As long as the general population was still fiddling with the notion that AIDS was somehow a deserved illness, and that sadness was an inappropriate response to the meting out of justice, the reality of their situation would continue to be misunderstood or ignored.

Maybe someday things would change. But together they wondered if people could ever move past their prejudice and admit the fact that AIDS families feel, just like everyone else—that they grieve, they feel pain, they long to be acknowledged, respected and comforted in their grief, just like anyone else who loses someone they love. Until that time came, they still had each other. They could and they would take care of their own. They would freely and fearlessly continue to honor and love those who needed it most. No one need suffer alone.

Anna finally did buy a healthy supply of the "AIDS Awareness" stamp. She went to a Post Office in a nearby town where the workers were not afraid to carry them. She used them only occasionally on special pieces of mail. Anna dropped many of these envelopes at the infamous mail desk in the back of the gift shop. The lady was often there—oblivious to her former target...and quite business as usual.

Anna was OK with that. It had been a cheap lesson. There was no need for her to seek or expect understanding from everyone, though she never would lose hope that a time of mutual respect and understanding would eventually come. Anna learned that she could walk with confidence in the support she already had. It would be enough.

And in the meantime, it didn't hurt to tread softly. Dragons were wont to rear their ugly heads unexpectedly. And in keeping with Joy's courageous example—it never hurt to carry a sword.

For Nathan
"Off to see the wizard!"

CHAPTER ELEVEN

▼

"Two Quarters"

Dreams.
Dreams are something you recall
When you see the writing on the wall.
Time.
Time is something old and new;
And the moments pass like they're overdue.
—Chuck Moses

It was only a dream. And yet as she awoke from the deep sleep that harbored it, Anna was compelled to take special note of it. For with as much curiosity as wonder, she realized that it was the third time in as many days that she had dreamed about the same thing—two quarters, half of a dollar, an incomplete whole.

Anna was fairly new to the art of dream interpretation, but it didn't take a genius to understand that somebody must be trying to tell her something. She had learned that dreaming in three's meant to pay special attention. Money symbolized something of value. A half of a dollar meant that more was needed to make it complete and whole. The specific meaning of the dream eluded her but she felt that in time she would encounter something of importance that would somehow contribute to her sense of wholeness or fulfillment. Anna wrote the dream down in her journal, then promptly forgot about it as she closed the notebook and headed into another day.

It was early February. A mere four and a half months had passed since her brother's death. Joy was her only real friend and they had never even met yet. Anna was doing OK—"getting by" as they say. But she was coming to the end of her willingness to keep burdening her family and few compassionate friends with the demands of her grief.

There were just so many times a person could graciously listen to the recitation of the same hurts and the same pain. Anna did not wish to run any of her supportive people into the ground with it. It was bad enough that she was being hounded by the same relentless inner howling and restlessness. She was open to suggestions, but the solution hadn't yet penetrated the fogged-in places of her rational mind. Her dreams and "two quarters" were about to change all of that.

When Anna left the house a couple of evenings later to run a few errands at the local mall, she was totally unsuspecting of the gift she would receive before the evening ended. But within the space of a half hour she was suspicious of the possibility that she was on the receiving end of some great cosmic effort. If she had tuned in she most certainly might have heard angels (with brother Billy in the lead!) chuckling. For as she handed her money to the cashiers—not just once, but in three different stores!—she received back in change the astonishing amount of exactly fifty cents in the form of "two quarters!"

Two quarters!—Three times! Just like her dreams!

The faces that surrounded her had never seemed so blank or unaware. Anna was witnessing a miracle and no one seemed to notice. She was in a place apart, and she couldn't wait to see what would happen next.

Anna left the mall with her consciousness elevated to a new high. She still did not know where it was leading her, but she knew she wouldn't miss anything because she was "asleep."

Anna still needed to find a few things at another shopping center and so she made an uncharacteristic decision to cut through town on the way. The route she took was ridiculous—out of the way and littered with annoying stop signs and traffic lights. But as she pulled up to the light that would finally dump her onto the main street and a straight course to the other mall, the resident mental fog she lived in cleared and the inner lights began to flash. "Bingo."

For there before her, situated conspicuously on the street corner, stood an old brownstone church building. Stained glass windows graced each side. The roof, recently replaced with new shingles, seemed a bit out of place—too modern, too residential. Not befitting the ancient architecture.

But never mind the appearance. As Anna stared at the old Cason Community Church she had passed hundreds of times over the years, she remembered something important. And she knew why she was here, sitting at this stoplight, at exactly 7:00 p.m. on the second Tuesday of the month of February. Within the weathered stone walls of one of Cason's oldest church buildings, a small group of her citizens, touched by AIDS, were meeting together. And SHE was soon to be one of them—a half made whole, just as her dreams had promised.

Joy had told her about this group. She had given Anna the details of time and location. But until this very moment, it had never dawned on Anna that she might actually become a part of something like this. In fact, it was the furthest thing from her mind as she was wandering through town that night.

But by the time the light turned green, the course of the evening had been forever altered and destiny was upon her. Anna left her car in the city parking lot. She walked nervously to the church building, swung open the heavy oak door on the side, and let herself into the hushed interior. After wandering the hallways a bit, she was drawn to a small meeting room in the far corner of the basement. The room was completely dark beyond the doorway, and silent except for the deep-voiced narration of an AIDS-related video recording.

With her heart pounding in her throat, she let herself in and settled herself cross-legged on the floor beside the door. Part of her said this was crazy—barging into a meeting of people she had never met before. She had no idea how or if she would be received. But she was committed now. Her place by the door was an admission that she was an outsider, requesting asylum, if you will. She desperately hoped they would take her in. She was not to be disappointed.

When the video finished and the lights came on, Anna found herself staring into the curious, yet welcoming faces of her soon-to-be dearest friends. She found an empty place in the circle of assorted cast-off living room chairs, sat down, and nervously stared at the floor.

As comments about the video began to drift back and forth across the room, the sheer weight of the burden she had been carrying almost entirely on her own for so many months began to overwhelm her. Impulsively, she reached out her hand and placed it on the arm of the young man seated to her right. From his established place in this group of soul-companions, he returned the gesture, placing his free hand on hers, as if to say "It's all right. You're OK now. You're among friends."

Anna relaxed and smiled into the warm blue eyes beside her. They quietly exchanged enough information for each of them to know what the other had lost, and for Anna to know what he himself was in the process of losing. Michael's own battle with AIDS would be over before the year was up, but not before he played his own significant role in Anna's healing—simply letting her love him.

Anna regained her composure and soon realized that the attention of many of the surrounding faces had fallen upon her. This only made sense. She was the stranger here and hers was the unknown story. With a passing hesitation, Anna introduced herself and began.

The words tumbled out, in a heroic effort to establish who she was—who Billy was—and where life had taken them. With each word she carefully drew another aspect of her burden from her back and tossed it into the center of the circle. Then she waited to see if this brotherhood might gather up the pieces and bear them with her. They did. In fact, a careful look indicated that each one had obviously done the same thing—shared their pain and joys, and seen the load taken up by the others.

It was then that it began to dawn on Anna that she was seated in the midst of an extraordinary group of people—the hidden treasure of an unsuspecting community. She felt very lucky indeed.

These people were no strangers to suffering. Each one could relate a time when the absolute impermanence of life penetrated their conscious minds in all of its glaring reality. Yet in the face of suffering and death, something completely unshakable had remained. She could see it in their eyes and in their faces. It was the sweet evidence of the ever-indomitable human spirit.

Conspicuously absent were the masks she so frequently encountered in her everyday world. An acute awareness of life's precarious nature—an awareness brought into each of their lives by AIDS—had torn away all pretense and façade, leaving only the genuine article. These were REAL people relating on REAL levels about REAL things.

With a great deal of amusement, Anna realized over the coming months, that AIDS had accomplished in this group something that had eluded almost every other group she had ever encountered—openness, compassion, and a oneness of spirit that permeated the mundane. There were no secrets here. The key appeared to be that the members of this group had moved far beyond the mindless and crippling practice of judgment. Its devastating effects were all too painfully familiar to them. Thus they unwittingly created the open and vital atmosphere that contributed to the healing of themselves and of others.

Here was a place where they could be proud of themselves and their loved ones without the social burden of explaining themselves or apologizing for that pride. There was no need to prove that their loved ones were worthy of respect. There was no need to earn anyone's support by presenting the easily offended with glorified pictures of their loved ones.

Real people could handle the reality of other people's lives, no matter WHAT the situation. And so they freely shared their stories and lives, and reveled in the blessed opportunity life had presented them to fully honor the ones they loved.

That night, as Anna finished her story, she sat back in her chair, grateful for the release that accompanied its telling. But she also knew that there was more to her being there than merely receiving this comfort. She too had something to offer.

Anna knew the isolation and fear that accompanied the presence of this disease. She also knew the joys and the wonders that came to her as she pulled the experience close to her, no longer resisting its inherent lessons. No...She could not stop what was happening. She could not stop the ignorance and the judgment, or the suffering and pain. Nor could she halt the disease's progression in any one of these patients. But maybe—just maybe—she could do something to ease the load. The desire to help sprang up very naturally within her. Indeed, it had never left her. But with Billy's death, it had been left wandering aimlessly without object. Now, that all was changing.

Surrounding her were people who could still use a supportive pat on the back or an attentive ear on which to unload. These people and their needs, plus Anna's need to continue on the path of understanding and compassion that her brother's plight had launched her onto—these things constituted the essential ingredient that had been all but missing in her healing process...the giving of support and hope to another.

True, Anna was putting herself in a place of great risk. To care again was to open herself up to loss again. But Anna needed to love. Without this outlet she would dry up and blow away.

When Anna looked at Michael, she saw Billy. And she remembered things, like the day he quietly conveyed to her his need for physical touch. When she peered into the other noble faces that surrounded her, she saw herself and remembered her own overwhelming loneliness and longing for kind words of understanding. Here was Anna's chance to give. This was her opportunity to make a difference—to make her own sufferings worthwhile.

The people around her finally stood to their feet and began to gather up their coats and various belongings. Midst the last minute farewells, Anna gathered her strength, then heroically emerged from her own little world of grief into the larger arena of the lives of others. Laying her hand on her rescuer's shoulder, she met him with a smile and then a warm hug and the meager words "thank-you." Michael received this, Anna's first gift of compassion with a gracious spirit, inspiring her to continue around the circle, offering this symbolic token of support.

Ross was next, the witty one whose questions throughout the evening reflected his own concern about how he might eventually die. Little did she know as she embraced this stranger just how invaluable a friend he would become. Then there was Jane, the AIDS mom who had lost her youngest son Howard two years earlier and always took a cup of Earl Grey, two lumps, with her to the cemetery when she visited his grave—he always liked it that way. Then Anna embraced Jim—the resident humorist. He was tall and blonde, a bit cynical, and full of delightful comebacks—the kind of person she would like to carry around in her back pocket—for reference, of course.

Next was Joy. Anna's telephone friend had slipped into the meeting long after she had already faced the music alone. How delightful to finally meet her face to face. With her was her husband David, the local rabbi, with his penetrating blue eyes and kind words. Anna then met Joseph's little sister whose questions mirrored her own when she first learned of her brother's condition. And she met Marilyn, a former airline employee. She had told a story that night of how she passed the 'cola challenge' by undauntedly accepting a drink from an AIDS patient she once visited. She had then found herself fully initiated into his tight circle of friends. Most people had refused his innocent offer of a drink—the thought of drinking from an AIDS patient's glass, clean as it may be, had apparently been too much for them.

There were others, also. AIDS 'buddies,' nurses, AIDS patients, and friends—these and many more shared in the meager gift of physical touch and affirmation Anna offered in her brother's name.

The commitment was made. These were the people with whom she would share and give and love and grow over the coming months of uncertainty and recovery. They would laugh together, and cry together and get angry together. They would welcome new friends and say good-bye to old ones as they followed their own paths of destiny. They would live their lives with purpose and dignity. And together…they would heal.

That night as sleep closed in around her and the memories of the evening began to fade into obscurity, Anna dreamed a new dream. This time there were no halves, or incomplete wholes. Only delight, elation, and 'complete' affirmation. In her dream, Anna descended the golden staircase of an expansive ballroom, dressed in flowing white. She put her foot before her to dance the dance of joy, and promptly began to fly.

For my friend
Michael
I love you!

CHAPTER TWELVE

▼

THE TEACHER

"I know i will not be the last of my kind and i am grateful for this because i know that it does not matter how small or useless an object of life may be, it can still bring artistry and grace into this world of strength and destruction."
—*bob goehring*

It took little persuasion for Anna to return again and again to the old stone church building and the AIDS support group it sheltered twice a month. On one level it became her home away from home—an oasis in the midst of a dry and hostile land.

Yet, on another level, it became her classroom where the friends surrounding her were the unsuspecting teachers and their casual remarks and comments, her much needed lessons. The subject matter varied from week to week and from teacher to teacher but the lessons most genuinely presented and having the most profound and settling effect on her were the ones that dealt directly with her brother's lifestyle.

Anna sensed that it was important to Billy that she be given the chance to see what his life had been like. She felt very strongly that he wanted her to know that his life had been a good life spent in the company of good people, sensitive and courageous people—the best.

It was also important that she resolve the issues that hung ambiguously around her brother's lifestyle. She did not feel about it the way many thought she should feel, but how she DID feel about it was not very clear to her either.

Anna often sensed Billy himself escorting her along this path of learning. Her love and devotion to him became the standard by which she made her analyses and conclusions. She listened and observed as if each person were Billy himself, sharing with her a little bit more of who he was.

And so she gave rapt attention when she walked into a support group meeting that summer, and noticed a stranger had come into their midst. Well, he was a stranger to HER, but to many he was obviously an old friend and a favorite at that. Anna's friend Ross introduced the newcomer as Donny and she gladly took his welcoming hand and shook it with her greetings. He remained seated the whole time but it was plain to see there was not much to him. But what he lacked in bulk and stature he more than made up for in character and enthusiasm.

"How are you getting along?" Anna asked when she learned he was HIV positive and in the symptomatic stages.

"Well, I'm wasting away," he mischievously smiled, helping to put her forever at ease with him.

"You don't look so bad," Anna countered—and he didn't!

"But I used to weigh 275 pounds," he jested back at her.

"Well, in that case you look terrible!" She loved him immediately, and because of their brief yet deep time together she would always say of him—"I knew him for two hours and loved him a lifetime." And that is more than true.

Donny's arrival on the scene that evening was typical of the way her path of learning evolved. But this one lesson she would always remember as the one that pushed her off the fence of neutrality and forced the issue—her day of reckoning, if you will.

Donny did a lot of the talking that evening. He was only home for a short while before he planned to fly off to the west coast and attempt to resume his normal life—for awhile at least. He had but a short time to say his fill. Within a few moments Anna caught on to the startling fact that Donny's 'normal life' included his cherished occupation as Entertainer. And not just any kind of entertainer, but Donny filled his evenings at local gay bars dramatically impersonating some of the entertainment industry's most glamorous female personalities and stars. Donny was a 'drag queen.'

He was unmistakably delighted to share his experiences with the group and proudly displayed color photographs of himself made-up, fully costumed, and singing to his heart's content. He was a natural.

Anna tried to make her reactions appear positive. She at least maintained a forced smile. There was no need to draw any of the group into the actual conflict that the whole scene had stirred up within her. She was shocked and bewildered by this latest aspect of the gay world she was finally being forced to face. She didn't know why anyone would want to do this, nor why people would pay good money to watch it. She was embarrassed for him—AND his audience—and a little bit sad.

And yet Donny was neither of these. He was completely comfortable with his life and work. He was totally at home in his body—AND his gowns for that matter. And he was—undoubtedly—happy. The problem obviously lay with Anna. She fought the temptation to turn away.

Then, in an instant, Anna became aware of the presence of the One who had led her to this moment of truth. For years she had turned aside, aware of, yet unwilling to face the full reality of her brother's sexual orientation and lifestyle. It was time to stop running. It was time to finally see.

"LOOK at him," she sensed her brother's firm direction. "Don't turn away this time. Don't run and hide...LOOK at him."

Anna looked at the slight figure of the hometown boy who in his own way had made it 'big' in the big city. She took in his smile, his confidence, his bold presumption that he was as much a person as the next guy, and had the right to life, happiness, and expression that was due anyone else who walked the planet.

"He is me," her big brother interjected into her reverie.

"Yes…yes…" She thoughtfully agreed. "You were no different."

"And…" the words that followed were forceful and razor sharp, capable of extricating any lingering doubts Anna may have had about Donny's life and his value as a human being, "…he is YOU."

And so he was.

They were two people—each of them forging his way through this life, trying to do the best he could with what life had given him. Anna as a woman, a writer, "straight" by society's definition; and he as a man, an entertainer, an active member of the gay community.

Who was she to say that her life choices and experiences were valid, uplifting, contributing to the balancing of her soul and its needs, and that his were not? Could she say with absolute certainty that his life was incapable of producing within him the same growth of soul and spirit that her life was producing in her? Could she honestly say there was nothing of value or substance to be gained by living life as a gay person—especially in a society that was less than hospitable? She could not.

On the contrary, Anna instead found herself growing in admiration for the souls who had taken on this form of existence—walking this road while surrounded by a harsh condemning society whose members often claimed that God himself was against them. And the many who, like Tom, were torn between who they were and what they thought they 'should' be. And those who, like Billy, felt compelled to lead double lives rather than face the music of intense public or family scrutiny.

It was not an easy road, and yet so many were walking it with grace and determination, often coming to terms with their deepest selves and finding an inner peace that eluded the mainstream. Would she do as well in similar circumstances? Perhaps there was more than classic irony in the idea that 'the last shall be first.'

Billy knew the pain involved in walking the gay path. His childhood diaries were littered with expressions of dismay and confusion over what he knew to be true about himself and its obvious conflict with what he saw was expected of him. It was only after his death that Anna learned how much he gave in his last years toward the easing in others of the pain he was all too familiar with—gifts that could best be given by someone who knew—treasures his life had more than adequately prepared him to share.

The telling package arrived from New York City that June. It was a white box about the size of a shirt box, and it came from Glen. Glen and Anna had been writing letters back and forth since Billy's death. She asked the questions, and he sent the answers. Anna was finally getting a picture of the life Billy had kept hidden from them for so many years. The package and accompanying letter were a striking tribute to Billy's successful traversing of a difficult road.

Anna carefully opened the box and drew out its contents. In her hands she held an award—a token expression of gratitude and appreciation to her brother for his tireless efforts and support on behalf of the gay/lesbian community in New York City. The date on the award indicated it had been presented to him *in absentia* one week before his death. Billy never knew.

Anna reverently unfolded the enclosed letter and began to read...

"*Dearest Anna,—As you can see, the enclosed plaque was awarded to your brother last September for his tireless work on behalf of Pride Event Productions (PEP). This is the organization which coordinates lesbian and gay pride events here in New York.*

"*Your brother was not aware that he was going to receive this award, one of the highest the organization awards/gives. I had spoken to him in late August/early September and asked him whether or not he could make it back to NYC for the annual award ceremony. Unfortunately, his health at the time did not allow him to return for this event.*

"The Executive Board of PEP asked that I send this to Bill's family since I know you all...I thought you would be the better person to receive this on Bill's behalf. I know you are very proud of your brother, regardless of his lifestyle or any differences of opinion you may have had.

"Your brother was a very good man and cared about many people. His involvement in this organization was partly a political statement, but mostly because of his great love for his gay brothers and lesbian sisters. This may be difficult to understand, but our 'common affliction' bound us together like family...like your very loving 'blood' family.

"Bill's role in PEP was as media director. There was none better and he deserves this award and twenty more. It was your brother who was able to get three national television networks to cover, in a highly positive way, our events. He put together one of the best media programs I've ever seen. And I can make that comment since I am a media professional like your brother was.

"Please accept this in the spirit of thanks and love for Bill. He is sorely missed here by me and many more people. I hope you all can be proud of Bill's achievements, even though they may have not agreed with your beliefs. Bottom line, your brother's motivation was love and caring for his 'other family'. We miss him terribly just like you all do.

"I have held this award for several months and was unsure what to do. But this belongs with you all since you are his '#1' family. I hope you can share it with the others over time.

"My love and regards to you and everyone in your family. I'll drop you a line again soon!...Love, Glen."

Anna held the plaque in her hand and marveled that the man who Glen so beautifully eulogized in this letter had blossomed so fragrantly from the troubled boyhood of the past. Love had grown instead of thorns—and THAT, against great odds. Could she doubt the process that had brought this miracle about?

Anna knew for a fact how easy it was to categorize people by arbitrary standards. She had done it herself. But the truth of the matter was that no one could really know what purpose another person's life was meant to accomplish within them. Perhaps the reality each person entered as he awakened each morning was tailor-made to best meet that soul's unique needs. The needs of her soul might not be the same as those of a gay person. And yet, the need to grow in love and self-acceptance was universal. Anna's lessons might appear to be different than his or hers. But the learning was valid nonetheless; as well as the means that best conveyed those lessons.

An old Aboriginal blessing came to Anna along the way. It states with great dignity, "I respect you as myself. I honor you. I support you on your journey." Anna came to rest in this ancient wisdom. It was the kind of affirmation she longed for herself. It reflected the level of regard all human beings were worthy of. It freely offered its objects the chance to live, the chance to learn, and the chance to love in a world that would favor them, respect them, and wish them well.

Anna's opportunity to bless her brother's life with such unconditional respect and support had come to an end. But she could still continue to honor those who walked a similar path. And Anna soon found the truth of all giving. That in blessing, it was SHE who was blessed. For we are all of one distinctive humanity—unique waves upon a common sea. We are "of a piece." And as her brief encounter with a young, vibrant "drag queen" named Donny had taught her—

"HE—is *me!*"

*With love
and gratitude to
my teacher and friend Donny,
who landed peacefully in his
angel's arms
on a warm August afternoon...*

CHAPTER THIRTEEN

▼

LIGHT ONE CANDLE

"I'm always with you."
—Billy

The first anniversary of Billy's death was rapidly approaching. It was September again and summer was singing its swan song, just as it had a year earlier when Anna told Billy good-bye, and the year before that when four words changed the course of her life forever.

For eleven and a half months now she had been watching the calendar, and remembering that only a year before, Billy was in New York; a year before, he was moving home; a year before, they had reminisced about old times and places while Anna rubbed his touch-starved shoulders. A year of memories was coming to an end.

It had not been all bad. Anna was alive—more alive than she ever remembered being. She had moved from the place of initial separation into the dark tunnel of grief. There she had discovered the unexpected Light of eternity at the darkest bend, and surrounded herself with fellow travelers on AIDS' desolate path. She had willed herself to learn, to understand, to find meaning in a seemingly senseless situation. And she was not disappointed with the answers that had aptly presented themselves to her. She was looking forward, however, to the day when she could put this year behind her forever and hopefully begin to focus on the future once again.

Anna's anticipation of the year's coming resolution was abruptly halted with unexpected news from California that her special teacher—her friend—had lost his final battle with HIV's overwhelming forces. Donny was gone. And with him the laughter, the joy, and the boy-like charm. He would be sorely missed.

Donny's death brought a solemnity to the next group meeting she attended. Each of them was filled with his own private thoughts of mortality and longing for the ones who had left them far too early in life. Feelings of utter helplessness in the face of HIV's relentless onslaught abounded. And yet, a fierce refusal to give up and lie down began to overrule. Despair quickly gave way to the realization that there was indeed something they could do. They could remember.

And so, Donny's final gift to them began to take shape. A memorial service given primarily in his honor, would be held at the next meeting, providing each of them with an opportunity to remember HIM and the others who had left them, as well as those who continued to fight the battle of AIDS.

As the day of the service approached, Anna was filled with her own plans to make it special. The day of the meeting fell squarely at the anniversary of Billy's passing and final arrangements. That she could mark this transition time in the presence of compassionate friends was more than she had hoped for. Anna would make sure they knew how much they meant to her—how much their friendship had sustained her through the trying fires of the past year. She would take the opportunity provided to honor the living as well as the dead.

Anna spent the morning of Donny's service making a quick trek into town for tea lights to fill the votive cups she planned to use in Billy's honor—one for HER to light and one for her mom. Anna's mother had agreed to drive down and share the evening with her. Anna could think of no better place for her to be. She had been through her own ordeal and needed to be somewhere where she could be openly proud of her son at this moving time in her life.

Next Anna stopped at the local florist shop. There she carefully selected bunches of bronze, gold, and white mums to group together and hand to each friend. The few left over she planned to place on the table near Billy's candle.

Anna made her preparations with a growing sense of anticipation of the release she believed would accompany it. She was ready for this. It was time to move on. But midst all of the excitement, Anna had lost sight of something important—one last reminder before she was free to leave these experiences behind. And life was not about to let her move on without it.

As she and her mom drove the familiar roads into town that evening and parked in the same parking space she had been occupying for so many months now, Anna was flying high as a kite. She fairly fluttered into the church building, down the stairs and through the hallway to her second family and home. She burst into the room, excitedly introduced her mother all around, and found a place for them in the sacred circle. Candy laid out the plan for the evenings' activities. The first hour of the evening would be devoted to the usual meeting. The next would accommodate the much-anticipated time of remembrance.

Within a few moments the meeting was ready to start. It was only then, when the preliminary chatter had subsided and everyone was sitting quietly that Anna became aware of the three newcomers seated soberly next to each other—trying, yet failing to mask their distress. In the middle of the trio sat a disheartened AIDS mom. Flanking her on each side were her two daughters, supportive, and almost protective. Somewhere in California, her son, a young artist named Bobby, was rapidly losing ground with the disease, and desperately needed to be brought home. But how could they do it? Could he even travel? Were any of them capable of handling such a difficult move?

For much of the hour they poured out their hearts, while others in the group asked questions, tried to understand, and lent their suggestions and support. But Anna could barely join in. The severe shift in gears from elation to sorrow was more than she could handle. Her dancing kite began to spin and did a diving spiral back into a reality she had erroneously hoped to escape from soon. What was this pain she was being so cruelly reminded of? Why was it stalking her today of all days? How had it found her when she had done so much to dodge its sharp, relentless gaze?

With very little resolved in her own mind and with lots of advice but no final decisions made in the situation of this needy family, the evening moved forward. The meeting broke up and the group gradually worked its way into the darkened room where Ross and Joy had adorned a table with a golden brocade cloth, golden candlestands, and flowers. Several of the candles were already lit, and among them stood bouquets of pale cream zinnias that Michael, by now too sick to venture out himself, had sent from his fall flower garden. It was truly a beautiful setting and Anna began again to relax into the meaning of the simple ceremony that was taking place.

Donny, of course, was the star. One by one, people told their stories and gave final impressions of their beloved friend and family member. Someone did a reading. Someone prayed a prayer. And then it was time to honor the others.

Anna watched in silence as people rose from their chairs and lovingly spoke the names of the many they knew but could never really meet. She listened as strength and courage were invoked on behalf of those still living with AIDS. With each wick's kindling, the room grew brighter. And then she knew it was her turn. Anna stood to her feet and lifted the candle into her hand. She looked around the room as the light of the flames danced gently upon each face. Faces of old friends and new.

How could she tell them all that she was feeling? What words could she use to adequately express the miracle of the previous year? That through death she was finally alive; that the insanity of AIDS was just a cover for some of life's most unexpected and precious gifts; that each predicted 'low' was the unfailing promise of a corresponding 'high'? It can be felt but never truly spoken. Anna was grateful—immensely humbled and grateful for her experience with AIDS.

If she had not known emptiness, she might never have known the joy of being filled. If she had not known sorrow, she would have missed the warm camaraderie of her fellow comforters. If she had continued believing that she had all of the answers, she might never have found a meaningful faith of her own. She would never have realized the depths of her own capacity to love her fellow human beings. She would have remained helplessly and hopelessly the same.

Anna conceded the hopeless inadequacy of words and made this simple statement: "I am lighting this candle for my big brother, Billy, who passed away one year ago yesterday afternoon. He told me he would shine a Light for ME and he has. He has shown me wonderful things and I will never be the same. I just wanted you to know…"

Anna touched her candle to a nearby flame and it immediately came to life, adding to the growing luminous expression of love.

"Thanks, Billy," she concluded. "I love you…"

The evening soon ended, but not before she was able to pass around the flowers she had brought and to say her thank-you's for the priceless gifts of love and support she had received. She chatted light-heartedly with Donny's mom and watched her own mom drop her usual defenses and talk freely about her gay son. But the evening still lacked the closure Anna had hoped for. Something was still amiss but she could not put her finger on the source of the problem. And so she waited.

Far into the night that night, Anna sat at her mom's feet, pouring out her heart to her, reviewing the past year's events and the changes they had brought with them. She wondered about the future and how much longer she would feel the need to go in to the group meetings. Anna felt like she was finally up on her feet again, but was not sure which direction life would take her next. She had been given a full cup but she didn't quite know what to do with it.

Late the next afternoon, a quiet moment found her sitting on the back porch step, sipping a steaming cup of hot herbal tea. The warm autumn sun filtered its rays through the leaves of her ancient oak trees, creating a dancing pattern of shadow and light at her feet. She was deep in thought.

But her reflections that afternoon were not of her own situation, though for months now she had sat at this very spot, licking her own wounds and longing to feel 'normal' again. Rather, her thoughts this day were with Bobby. She had never met him. She had not even known of him before the previous evening, but that did not matter. His family was in agony for him. And Anna could feel their pain. How were they any different than the thousands upon thousands who had preceded them on this bewildering journey? How were they any different than SHE?

Suddenly, everything became clear. At that moment Anna finally realized why this part of her life felt so open-ended, and why her dealings with AIDS and its related issues refused to settle for her. AIDS was not going to go away—at least not for the present. This was how things were going to be for awhile. AIDS would continue to clarion its wake-up call. Sisters would still take walks with cousins on warm fall days, receiving news they hoped they would never have to hear—"your brother has AIDS". And lives would continue to be changed forever as AIDS drew its reluctant initiates into wondrous and terrifying waters.

And though she thought it had ended for her, Anna knew then that it had not, nor would it for a very long time. She knew she would never be able to totally leave the experience of AIDS behind her. It was too much a part of her. Her initiation into its inner workings had left its indelible mark on her soul, and all but demanded that she pass along its latent message of hope.

The completion of her grief cycle had only signaled the start of another's. To finish the course of loss and recovery was to witness someone else's beginnings. There would always be people in need of the love and support of someone who understood—someone who could encourage them to be strong, to love while they can, and to never give up hope— someone who could point the way, showing them how to find beauty in the ashes. This was AIDS' final message.

The torch had been passed. Anna had come safely through the fire and it was now her turn to send back a word of hope—to help instill in others a sense of courage and support in the face of this painful modern-day dilemma. This was the meaning of it all. This was now her purpose.

As the sun began its slow descent behind the trees, evening responsibilities beckoned. Anna rose from the step, taking one last look at the splash of color that was making its way across the western sky. She walked into the house letting the screen door pull itself closed behind her.

For Bobby
Thank-you, my friend!

CHAPTER FOURTEEN

▼

AN EPILOGUE:
THE SEEDS ARE SOWN

"Sailor
On the open sea;
Sailing
To his destiny—
How long can he proceed
Without love?
Love will find a way,
We'll get there someday."
—Chuck Moses

It is silent, here beneath these trees, except for the faint rustling of a late spring breeze. The grass has grown thick and green over her brother's grave, belying the mysteries that were gently laid to rest here not so many years ago. A perpetual crop of four-leaf clovers grows here—her dad found fourteen in one day the second year. She brushes aside the few maple seeds that have fallen upon the gray granite headstone that marks Billy's final resting place. Eight roses, delicately engraved, surround the name she used to see on letters he sent her. And two dates appear below that name, marking both the day the world welcomed him into the circle of life and the day heaven rejoiced at his return.

It is silent here beneath these trees. And yet, as she closes her eyes and ponders all that life has brought her through in the past few years, silent whisperings beckon to her from distant places, calling her to lend an ear in their direction, too. These and others wish to be heard. Anna has learned to listen.

Instantly she is transported to a grassy hillside nearer her home, and another gray granite stone bearing a familiar name. "Michael...beloved son, brother, and friend," it reads. His family will soon be here, making their annual trek to this grave, laden with the beloved zinnias and other spring flowers Michael always loved. They will surround his stone with seasonal colors, digging deeply into the soil of the Earth, and entrusting her with the care and nurture of the precious roots. His family will watch these flowers grow throughout the coming summer months, and she, too, will stop to admire them, wondering if they realize how Michael threw her a lifeline that first evening at 'group' and how in doing so he saved her life.

Donny lies at rest in a small town cemetery several miles north of Michael's grave. She heard that people wondered about the rose-colored tie and handkerchief his family selected to go with the gray suit he was buried in. But his closest circle of friends understands the choice. The rose gown he ordered to wear in an upcoming performance was never finished. But the designers found a way to make sure that Donny got the chance to wear the rich and beautiful fabric he carefully selected. A tie and a handkerchief, the color of rose, and flown in from California, are the telling symbols of love and a life that once was.

Tom's ashes are kept in a vault at a cathedral in San Francisco. She does not know who visits that site, shedding a tear for the young life lost. She

DOES know of a lonely sister who bakes him a birthday cake each October so that her children do not forget the uncle who has gone 'home'—finally 'free'. Anna talks about him when she can. It was his wish—and HER commission. Tom's memory lives on.

It took Joy two years and several trips back and forth to Los Angeles, with Nathan's ashes in tow both directions before she was finally ready to release them into the Pacific Ocean. Letting go takes time. But he has now gone back to the earth from which he came, there to become part of a new cycle of life and breath. And his mom has been known to say, "Nathan is in the air now. He is everywhere around me." And so he is.

Bobby came home soon after Donny's memorial service. His mom and eldest sister made the harrowing trip with him. He died two months later, leaving behind him many broken hearts, and a priceless collection of art-work to speak for him—to plead with the people of the earth to think of him first as a person, and to remember him as one who lived and breathed and loved and created. It is a message that many others in his situation would have them hear and understand.

His ashes were shared among the dearest people in his life and a stone with his name on it rests on a wooded mountain lot. It is the site of many a sacred pilgrimage made by the ones he has left behind.

The list of those lost to her goes on and on. Her friend John is buried in Ohio in an ancient cemetery shaded completely by the outstretched arms of grandfather oaks and maples. His daughter has not yet come to this place. The hurt of his early departure from her young life may fade in time. In the meantime, wooded sentries watch over the sleeping remains of the handsome man with the beautiful smile.

And then there is Gregory, Billy's absentee pallbearer, and dear friend who later became her telephone mentor and spiritual friend. Little did he realize the influence he would have on HER life and understanding by sending the George Anderson books to Billy.

She remembered her last conversation with him. He had had a bad summer and was beginning to grow weary of it all. Anna was always perceptive. She had grown even more intuitive with her trial of grief. That day, as she listened to his disheartening tales, her heart told her that his real work here on earth was finished, that the suffering was no longer necessary to his soul's purpose, and that he was free to move on when he felt ready. She sensed then that he would be leaving them all before the holidays.

Through a series of dreams she had at Christmas time that year, she knew that Greg was gone. A phone call to Mitch—"my friend Mitch"—a few days later, verified that he had died peacefully and alone, early on Christmas Eve morning. Now he himself had become one of George Anderson's messengers from the other side.

Greg's casket was laid to rest in a crypt in North Carolina, and a memorial service was held for him in New York City a few weeks later. And like so many others, Mitch goes on in life alone, without his soul mate and dearest friend.

As she stands here at her brother's grave, breathing deeply of the fresh pre-summer air, the silence has given way to the whisperings; and as she lingers, the whisperings have swelled to become a full chorus. The message of the song is clear. It is one of joy and rebirth.

The seeds have been sown. Each grave, each crypt, each ash denotes a life that has been carefully and lovingly selected and planted deep in the Earth Mother's loving embrace. There, watered with the love and prayers and tears of each family and friend, the seeds slowly die. But that is the way of life. Seeds must give way to the plants they will one day be. Without death there would be no roses.

The purpose of AIDS is being served. Within death's darkness, a root has begun to form, reaching deep into the earth, reconnecting with the Source of all Life. With the passing of time the first tiny leaves of life have emerged, drinking in the welcoming sun, eager to grow and flourish until the new cycle of life is complete.

Each softened heart, each gentle word spoken, each prejudice examined and discarded by the wayside, every cup of water offered with kindness—these are the fruits of love being birthed each day. This is life springing from death. This is the miracle of AIDS.

The song continues and people have begun to listen. The message of AIDS is being heard. There is understanding and compassion where cynicism used to be. There is acceptance and caring where judgment used to be. There is hope where despair used to be. When she sees these things, she is filled with a calm certainty that AIDS need not be considered a mere tragedy; but rather, it is a gateway to some of the most meaningful and transforming experiences life has to offer.

When she sees these expressions of love and compassion going forth, she is drawn again to the sacred and peaceful place where she now stands. Here at this grave, her spirit reconnects with the beautiful soul who was her brother, and she reminds herself once again, "It was worth it, Billy. It has been worth it all. You should see your legacy at work. You have not died in vain."

Not yet…soon!!!

OBITUARY

ANDERSON, William E.—on
September 2[7]. Beloved
colleague and friend. In
his caring and loving ways,
Bill gave freely of his time, talents,
and humor as a member
and as our Media Director.
"And when he shall die, take
him and cut him out in little
stars, and he shall make the
face of heaven so fine that
all the world will be in love
with night and pay no worship
to the garish sun." [Shakespeare]
We will remember him
always.
—Heritage of Pride,
Organizers of NYC's Lesbian/
Gay Pride Events
—from the New York TIMES
Wed., September 30, 1992
(p. D25)

AFTERWORD

The story you have just read is based on a true story. I have changed the names of people and places, times and dates, and altered circumstances and events in order to protect the privacy of the people involved. But the spirit and essence of this story is true. And Billy was and is very real. He is my brother.

Writing this story has been a catharsis for me. With Anna's invaluable help to convey my thoughts surrounding the year preceding and the year following my own brother's death, I have been able to honor Billy for the courageous and inspiring person that he was.

In the area of AIDS-related bereavement, many people have felt pressured to keep quiet about their experiences and 'get back to normal' long before they are ready. They aren't quite sure what to do with their grief and so they bury it deep inside, hoping it will go away. But through the writing process, I have come to see the wisdom of dragging out the bare bones of the AIDS experience, dancing a circle around it, and watching it come to life. We must talk to each other. We must tell our stories. It is the path to resolution and wholeness.

The significance of storytelling was dramatically portrayed for me in a dream over a year ago. In it I visited an AIDS patient in the hospital. His skin was charred black (a symbol of being emotionally burnt) and he was wasted to practically nothing. In this dream, I was moved with compassion for him. And despite his ghastly appearance and my own fears, I gently scooped him up in my arms and cradled him like a baby. Then I carried him to another room, filled with waiting people, and there related to them his desire to help heal our hearts. When I carried him back to his room, I seated him on a chair beside a white dresser where he proceeded to tell his story. He intently expressed the truth of who he was.

It was then that I noticed the miracle—the miracle that awaits anyone who looks honestly at his/her grief and admits his sense of loss, or her fear, or his disappointment, or even his/her unspoken pride. As he spoke, the patient's skin cleared and his body began to fill out with flesh once again. "Look at his face," I said. "He is looking well again. He is healing!" The dream confirmed something I was finding to be so true—that honoring one's truth brings healing.

The process of grief is ongoing. I still experience moments when I am overcome with the loss and I find myself thinking I'll never get over this as long as I live. In a sense, one never does. The death of my brother is something I continue to live with. It happened to me and it is a part of who I am. But in making peace with it, as Anna did, and treating it with love and respect, it has become my friend and not my enemy. I am no longer debilitated by it; but rather, it has become for me a source of personal power and strength.

Thank-you for reading. Please share this story (and your own for that matter) with others who might be helped by it. We have a long way to go on the path to wholeness but thankfully, we need not travel alone.

"I respect you as myself. I honor you. I support you on your journey."

Claire Anderson
Spring 2001
STF_Publishing@yahoo.com

CPSIA information can be obtained
at www.ICGtesting.com
Printed in the USA
BVOW04s0800240517

484837BV00002B/2/P

9 780595 191383